AUTHENTIC SPIRITUAL
LEADERSHIP

The Mega Church Corporate Model of the New Millennium

DR. PAMELA ALLEN

November 2011

authorHOUSE®

AuthorHouse™
1663 Liberty Drive
Bloomington, IN 47403
www.authorhouse.com
Phone: 1 (800) 839-8640

Published by AuthorHouse   03/18/2015

ISBN: 978-1-4969-7026-8 (sc)
ISBN: 978-1-4969-7027-5 (e)

Library of Congress Control Number: 2015902513

Print information available on the last page.

This book is printed on acid-free paper.

DEDICATION

———

    This authentic spiritual leadership series is dedicated to God who provided me with the vision, inspiration, motivation and sustainable strength to take this walk of faith. I give God all the praise for providing this opportunity to fulfill my purpose driven life and make a difference.

    I also offer dedication to all the family, friends, students, faculty, neighbors, Christian brothers and sisters that offered words of encouragement, prayers and a listening ear during the hard times. Because of the support of my extended family I know I was not alone in the valley.

    My prayer is that God will continue to use me as an instrument to produce fruitful and meaningful work that will bless all who believe that nothing is impossible. This is not the end of my journey but a new beginning

CONTENTS

———

Chapter 1: Introduction..1

Background of the Problem...2

Mega-churches..3

Statement of the Problem..4

Purpose of the Study...4

Significance of the Study...5

Significance to the Study of Leadership...5

Nature of the Study...6

Research Questions..7

Hypotheses..7

Theoretical Framework..7

Spiritual Leadership Theory...8

Definition of Spirituality...8

Spiritual Leadership..9

Mega-Church Organization...10

    Definition of Terms..10

Authentic Leadership...10

Mega-Church...11

Spirituality...11

    Assumptions...12

    Scope and Limitations..12

    Delimitations..12

    Summary...13

Chapter 2: Review of the Literature..15

Title Searches, Articles, Research Documents, and Journals...............................15

Internet Resources and Websites..16

Article and Scholarly Research Databases...16

Historical Overview of the Paradigm Shift...17

The Rational System Perspective..18

The Natural System Perspective 18

The Open System Perspective 19

Demonstrating Authentic Leadership 20

Spirituality in the Workplace 21

Historical Trends for Spiritual Leadership 23

Spiritual Leadership 23

Spiritual Leadership in Practice 25

Mega-Churches Mega-Corporations 26

Brief History of Lakewood Church 27

Conclusions 27

Summary 28

Chapter 3: Method 29

Research Method and Design Appropriateness 29

The Quantitative Method 30

Qualitative Research Designs 31

Correlational Research Designs 31

Research Question 32

Population 32

Sampling Frame 33

Informed Consent 33

Confidentiality 34

Geographic Location 35

Data Collection 35

Instrumentation 35

Revised Spiritual Leadership Survey 36

The Authentic Leadership Questionnaire 36

Validity and Reliability 37

    Validity 37

    Reliability 37

Data Analysis 38

Summary 38

Chapter 4: Results 39

Research Question and Hypotheses 40

Data Collection Procedures 40

Data Demographics 41

Data Analysis 42

Findings 46

    Hypothesis 46

Summary 47

Chapter 5: Conclusions and Recommendations..49
Conclusions...50
Hypothesis I...51
Leadership Implications...52
Recommendations..52
Recommendations for future research 53
Summary 54
References 55

CHAPTER 1

Introduction

Years of unethical leadership in almost every known business, church, and professional industry continue to plague the United States (U.S.) society. Scharmer (2009) stated, "Spiritual poverty describes the loss of connection to the collective body of humankind" (p. 82). Public scandals included the largest number of bankruptcy filings in U.S. history after discovery of unethical business practices (Thomas, Schermerhorn, & Dienhart, 2004). Highly visible organizational leaders demonstrating severe lapses in ethical judgment created public demands for greater accountability (Dealy & Thomas, 2006) including members of corporate boards (Aguilera, 2005). Inconsistent behaviors from executives increased risks for loss of trust and commitment from followers (Simons, 2002). AOL Time Warner, Duke Energy, Enron, Halliburton, Kmart, Qwest Communications International, Reliant Energy, Tyco, WorldCom, and Xerox are only a few entities known as fallen leaders among the industry (Fry & Slocum, 2008). Leaders who consider themselves models in the current work environment should demonstrate service, motivation, guidance, and encouragement in the midst of turbulence, conflict, innovation, and change (Kouzes & Posner, 2007). However, the current crisis in leadership indicates an abandonment of ethical business practices, standards of integrity, public accountability, and moral reasoning that influence individuals and groups to rationalize lies and deceit (Capps, 2003; Whittington, 2004). Spiritual leadership offers the new alternative for doing business in corporate America (Fry & Matherly, 2006). "The purpose of spiritual leadership is to create vision, and value congruence across the strategic empowered team, individual levels and, ultimately, to foster higher levels of organizational commitment and productivity" (Fry, 2003, p. 1). The new millennium will support development of spiritual intelligence that fosters ability to access authentic purpose and self (Scharmer, 2009). The mega-church is a new corporation of the 21st century, challenging leaders to join what Scharmer (2009) describes as a *cultural-spiritual* shift toward the rise of a new consciousness in models of leadership.

Therefore, additional discussions in chapter one will expand on reasons research regarding spiritual leadership is an important social concern. A specific statement of the problem will justify needs for the research study. Multiple sections will define the purpose of this study including research design, population, geographic location, significance, and nature of the study. The introduction will continue with clear identification of the primary research question, theoretical framework, and definition of essential terms. Rationalization of assumptions, scope, limitations, and delimitations provides the ability to develop a final summary of key points for chapter one.

Background of the Problem

The criteria assessing success and failure in corporate America are changing (Magnusen, 2002). Leaders in American businesses are searching for new leaders with the ability to transform organizations, resulting in what is good for the people and a revitalizing force establishing a sense of community and shared values (Magnusen, 2002). Trends in the workforce indicate officials from more Fortune 500 companies are incorporating spiritual and religious philosophies, models, and beliefs into their organizations (Fry & Whittington, 2005). For example, officials from three Fortune 500 companies that support the incorporation of spiritual leadership into existing organizational structures include TD Industries, Synovus Financial Corporation, and Southwest Airlines (Fry & Slocum, 2008).

Spiritual leaders establish a culture and environment for spirituality on multiple levels including organizational (Duchon & Plowman, 2005), individual, and team (Cacioppe, 2000a). Implementation of spiritual values into the organizational structure is evident in some of the most successful corporations in the United States including Southwest Airlines (Milliman, Ferguson, Trickett, & Condemi, 1999) and Starbucks (Marques, 2008). The new emphasis for leadership becomes moral development (Coles, 2000), authenticity (George, 2003), and spiritual maturity (Bolman & Deal, 2001; Sanders, Hopkins, & Geroy, 2003). The personal pursuit of spirituality transforms the contemporary work environment into a business practice that taps the human soul at work (Klenke, 2005). The U.S. worker re-defines value beyond simply receiving a paycheck for performance of tasks to living spirituality at work by experiencing a sense of purpose and meaning (Klenke, 2005).

The authors indicated that the workplace became the venue to express one's spirituality within a framework of worker empowerment and shift to participative management style (Elmes & Smith, 2001). American employees expend a large amount of time, physical, mental and emotional energy in the work environment. Considering other activities of daily living, the workplace becomes a substitute for meaningful relationships with family and friends (Elmes & Smith, 2001).

The transformation begins with supporting new standards of corporate integrity, accountability, and ethical and moral responsibility. Spiritualizing the workplace expands significantly as spiritually based organizations transform into spiritual corporate cultures around the nation (Wagner-Marsh & Conley, 1999). The new age approach to spirituality impacts the focus on spiritual leadership within the growing mega-church movement.

Mega-churches

Irwin and Roller (2000) suggested that as contemporary society becomes more diverse, educated leadership and management roles in the church were essential to organizational success. However, additional factors involve the success of the mega-church corporation. Hinton (2007) examined the theological and educational approach of two mega-churches. A primary assumption from Hinton's research study is that spiritual leadership is one factor contributing to mega-church growth.

Mega-churches resemble corporate structures attempting to address the best leadership practices, management strategies, and technological advances (Thumma, 2001). As an emerging organizational model, mega-churches appear to represent a "sense and respond" design (Herber, Singh & Useem, 2003, p. 40). Successful adaptation to unpredictable events and the ability to orient the entire organization around managing ongoing changes in customer needs and demands defines the mega-business entity (Mintzberg, Lampel, Quinn, & Ghoshal, 2003). Research suggests that transformations in a growing diverse culture and changes in the patterns of society describes a unique collective response towards forming mega-churches throughout industrialized, urban, and suburban areas of the world (Thumma, 2001).

According to Drucker (1999), mega-churches were the most important social phenomenon in the United States within the past 30 years. Drucker suggested that success for mega-churches appeared to be a combination of focus on spirituality and effective management of essential services instead of rituals. Mega-church management systems track finances and organize members with few staffers, audio-video tools enable competition for audiences amid popular culture, and telecom and web applications extend outside church walls to satellite campuses, allowing oversight of national church associations (Cone, 2005).

Researchers of a national study of approximately 1,200 mega-churches indicated a consistent organizational growth among mega-churches within the past eight years (Hartford Institute for Religious Research, 2008). According to Thumma and Bird (2008), mega-churches continued to grow in size with Protestant, multi-ethnic, congregation attendance of 2000 or more adults and children. Significantly, the mega-church environment attracts a large number of people (Thumma & Bird, 2008). Researchers at the Hartford Institute for Religious Research reported a 90% growth rate in mega-churches from 2000 to 2008. Recent researchers found a 50% increase in mega-church attendance during five-year periods with stagnation or decline occurring with only 10% of the churches (Thumma & Bird, 2008). As a sense-and-respond organizational design, mega-church response to environmental change indicates a larger number of worship services with expansion to multiple satellite locations. Focus on increasing participation in community service, decreasing use of radio and television and continuous development of the role of small groups adds definition to the sense-and-respond mega-church model (Thumma & Bird, 2008). Mega-church expansion results in additional benefits regarding significant increases in profit. Researchers suggest the average income for mega-churches was $6.5 million in 2008, representing an approximate increase of a half million dollars from 2005 (Thumma & Bird, 2008).

The church is a place of worship, spiritual growth, and illumination. However, the church is also a significant business requiring effective leadership, teamwork, and quality service. Evidence in the research literature supports organizational growth and profit among mega-churches. According to researchers at Hartford Institute for Religion Research (2008), size defined the mega-church. The average weekly attendance at mega-churches is 3,857 people (Thumma, 2001). Over the past 20 years, attendance at mega-churches increased by an average rate of 90% (Thumma, 2001). Thumma (2001) reported that based on the results of a study conducted in 1999 the average total annual income of mega-churches was $4.8 million. Recent researchers indicated the average income of mega-churches increased to $6.5 million (Thumma & Bird, 2008). Organizational growth targets the mega-church as a business phenomenon resulting in congregations of at least 2000 or more members and million dollar budgets (Thumma, 2001). Over the past 20 years, attendance at mega-churches increased by an average rate of 90%, and 83% of the church's dramatic growth occurred during the tenure of the senior pastor (Thumma, 2001). Still, little or no research exists, studying leadership practices associated with mega-church management.

Statement of the Problem

The general problem of the study concerned the current crisis in leadership. Abandonment of ethical business practices, standards of integrity, public accountability, and moral reasoning influenced individuals and groups to rationalize lies and deceit (Cashman, 2008). Highly visible organizational leaders demonstrated severe lapses in ethical judgment that created public demands for greater accountability (Dealy & Thomas, 2006). The specific problem investigated what constructs the spiritual and authentic leadership surveys actually measured. This quantitative study used a correlational research design that focused on comparing constructs in The Spiritual Leadership Survey and The Authentic Leadership Questionnaire to determine if the Spiritual Leadership Survey was a distinct measurement that identified spiritual leaders whose ethical, moral, and socially responsible behaviors could impact unethical leadership trends.

Purpose of the Study

The purpose of this quantitative correlational study was to determine if the same or different constructs exist within The Spiritual Leadership Survey and Authentic Leadership Questionnaire by surveying 100 volunteers at mega-churches located in Houston, Texas. The quantitative method selected was appropriate for this study because a quantitative method describes a problem that provides an explanation by obtaining an estimate or sample of a population, and discovering an association between variables (Cooper & Schindler, 2008).

The correlational design was appropriate because the research question driving this study involved measuring the degree of association among constructs. According to Cresswell (2005) correlational designs are procedures in quantitative research that measure degrees of association (or relationships) among two or more variables use statistical procedures of correlational analysis. Attempts to control or manipulate variables do not occur in correlational research designs because observations of variables occur as they exist naturally in the environment (Gravetter & Wallnau, 2005). The quantitative procedure involved administration of two existing survey instruments. Electronic data collection methods for each volunteer included an electronic version of the Spiritual Leadership Survey and Authentic Leadership Questionnaire sent to their personal e-mail address. The specific population was restricted to volunteers at each mega-church organization within Houston, Texas.

Significance of the Study

Spiritual leadership represents the new paradigm for organizational transformation (Fry & Matherly, 2006). A *cultural-spiritual* shift describes a new consciousness in the United States (Scharmer, 2009). The importance of the current study for post-modern organizations is an opportunity to explore how mega-church models demonstrate effective leadership, growth, and profit despite a downturn in the economy. Study of the spiritual leadership model may support efforts to identify factors contributing to the success of mega-churches as the fastest growing corporations in the United States. The current study is relevant for supporting a new paradigm that meets the needs of contemporary leaders and knowledge workers who plan to incorporate spirituality in the workplace. Milliman et al. (1999) addressed the significance of the positive impact of spirituality on employees and organizations considering that many chief executive officers (CEOs) will not support a recommendation without enhancing the bottom line. Information found by researching spiritual leadership provided empirical evidence supporting strong correlations between spiritual leadership, organizational growth, and profit. Research from the topic added to the existing literature supporting successful companies including Chick-Fil-A, Interstate Batteries, TD Industries, Southwest Airlines, Taco Bell, Pizza Hut, and BioGenenex, which currently incorporate spirituality into their organizational structures (Fry & Slocum, 2008; Mitroff & Denton, 1999). However, results from this study may also contribute significantly to the study of Leadership.

Significance to the Study of Leadership

Results from this research study offered significant contributions to the current study of leadership. Recent research by Caza, Bagozzi, Woolley, Levy and, Caza (2010) regarding psychological capital and authentic leadership revealed a positive correlation between the two constructs. Future research may include the addition of spiritual leadership with authentic leadership to determine if a correlation exists with psychological capital. According to Sarros & Cooper (2006) character and integrity represents the demand for a more sustaining type of leadership suggesting a shift away from visionary and charismatic leadership. The spiritual leadership model supports demonstration of character and integrity that contributes to sustainable leadership demands from society (Fry, 2008). Wong and Cummings (2009) support the trend toward authentic sustainable leadership that includes focus on relationships, foundation of morals and ethics, link to positive psychological capital, work engagement, leader, and follower development by stressing its importance in nursing leadership practice and changes in nursing work environments.

This study determined that weak to very weak associations existed among constructs within the Spiritual Leadership Survey and Authentic Leadership Questionnaire. Results from this study added support to essential elements in spiritual leadership that aligns with current and future leadership practices in a variety of disciplines. Jensen & Luthans (2006) explored the leadership practices of entrepreneurs and business founders in relation to authentic leadership. However, research regarding entrepreneurs would also benefit from employees perception of spiritual leadership as a predictor of job satisfaction.

However, Novicevic, Davis, Dorn, Buckley & Brown (2005) suggested a balanced perspective regarding conditions likely to result in inauthentic, pseudo-authentic or authentic leader behavior. Comparison of constructs between spiritual leadership and authentic leadership provided an opportunity to contribute to this balanced perspective by determining conditions likely to result in non-spiritual or pseudo-spiritual leadership behaviors. Walumbwa, Avolio, Gardner, Wernsing & Peterson (2008) suggested combining authentic, ethical, and transformational leadership into a training program that provides the best opportunities to impact long-term motivation and sustain high levels of performance. Spiritual leadership would be a significant addition to this recommendation to build leadership training programs consisting of the combined strengths of evolving leadership models.

Nature of the Study

A correlational analysis determined similarities and differences among constructs in The Spiritual Leadership Survey and Authentic Leadership Questionnaire by surveying a sample of 100 volunteers at mega-churches located in Houston, Texas. According to Creswell (2003), quantitative researchers sought causal relationships between variables, for prediction, and generalization of findings. The research problem for the study indicated no definitive evidence of a relationship among constructs found in The Spiritual Leadership Survey and Authentic Leadership Questionnaire. Some research problems in quantitative research involve correlations. Therefore, the most appropriate research design was a correlational analysis using appropriate data reduction techniques that determined the type, direction, and strength of relationships among variables. Simon and Francis (2004) cautioned researchers by emphasizing that the use of correlation studies does not determine cause and effect.

The quantitative method was appropriate for this research study because it provided an opportunity to explain any possible associations among constructs that included characteristics from The Spiritual Leadership Survey and Authentic Leadership Questionnaire. The research design provided a blueprint for main objectives to answer essential questions (Cooper & Schindler, 2008).

A correlational design was the optimum choice for this specific research to accomplish the goals for this study. According to Creswell (2005) investigators use correlational design procedures, in quantitative research, to measure degrees of association (or relationships) among two or more variables using statistical procedures. Attempts to control or manipulate variables do not occur in correlational research designs because observations of variables occur as they exist naturally in the environment (Gravetter & Wallnau, 2005).

Research Questions

The intent of the current quantitative research study was to determine if the same or different constructs existed in The Spiritual Leadership Survey and Authentic Leadership Questionnaire using a selection of volunteers located in mega-churches in Houston, Texas. Onwuegbuzie and Leech (2005) suggested that hypotheses began with a basic research question that allowed development of specific predictions about the nature of relationships between independent and dependent variables identified in the question.

From the statement of the problem, the following research question guided the study. What is the correlation, if any, among constructs in the Spiritual Leadership Survey (see Appendix A) and the Authentic Leadership Questionnaire (see Appendix B) for volunteers in mega-churches located in Houston, Texas. A quantitative research method included a correlational research design to compare constructs within The Spiritual Leadership Survey and The Authentic Leadership Questionnaire.

Hypotheses

From the research question, the null hypothesis was derived:

Ho: The Spiritual Leadership Survey measures different constructs than the Authentic Leadership Questionnaire for volunteers in mega-churches located in Houston, Texas.

The alternative hypothesis from the research question states:

H1: The Spiritual Leadership Survey measures the same constructs as the Authentic Leadership Questionnaire for volunteers in mega-churches in Houston, Texas.

The aim of the current research study was to determine if the Spiritual Leadership Survey and the Authentic Leadership Questionnaire measured the same or different constructs.

Theoretical Framework

The theoretical framework placed the current study in perspective among other relevant studies. An investigation of important issues and controversies regarding the spiritual leadership theory, definition of spirituality, spiritual leadership, and mega-churches added support to a broad theoretical area.

Spiritual Leadership Theory

Fry, Vitucci, and Cedillo (2005) suggested that "spiritual leadership theory is a causal leadership theory for organizational transformation designed to create an intrinsically motivated, learning organization" (p. 835). The authors concluded that spiritual leadership theory is the pathway toward a new paradigm and evolution in leadership theory, research, and practice (Fry et al., 2005). Spiritual leadership theory is an incorporation and extension of transformational, charismatic, ethics, and values-based theories such as authentic and servant leadership and "avoids the pitfalls of measurement model misspecification" (Fry et al., 2005, p. 835).

Fry et al. (2005) conducted additional research resulting in an extension of spiritual leadership theory to include concepts related to positive human health and well-being considering growing cultures of workplace spirituality. Ethical well-being defined the ability to be authentic while demonstrating personal and, professional values, attitudes and behavior from the inside out (Cashman, 2008). Current challenges to leaders are movement beyond external descriptions that focus on characteristics to inward reflections that reveal purpose and passion. Cashman (2008) also supported leading from the inside out by challenging leaders to move beyond "the outer manifestations of leadership (e.g. vision, innovation, results, drive, etc.) to the fundamental essence of leadership itself" (p. 23). According to Avolio (2008) leadership theory continues to evolve beyond what leader's do to who leaders are. Efforts to assess and explore the meaning of leadership in relationship to self and others are essential to significant growth and development (Avolio, 2008). Demonstrating results of inner explorations provides an opportunity to reveal authentic leadership (Cashman, 2008). Leading from the inside out creates opportunities to establish an ethical culture in the work environment with morals and social responsibility (Cashman, 2008). However, additional overview of the definition of spirituality is essential to the discussion.

Definition of Spirituality

Korac-Kakabadse, Kouzmin, and Kakabadse (2002) suggested a loose definition of spirituality in the literature focusing on energy, or meaning. In a review of the literature the preference for some scholars to choose Taoist, Buddhist, Hindu, Zen, and Native American spiritual perspectives, assuming that "non-Western societies are better in integrating personal life, work, leisure, prayer, religion and other aspects of one's life" (Korac-Kakabadse et al., 2002, p. 166). Heaton, Schmidt-Wilk, and Travis (2004) proposed a distinction between *pure* spirituality and *applied* spirituality by referring to "pure spirituality as silent, unbounded, inner experience of pure self-awareness, devoid of customary content of perception, thoughts, and feelings. Applied spirituality refers to practical applications and measurable outcomes that automatically arise from the inner experience of 'pure spirituality'" (p. 63).

In contrast, Elmes and Smith (2001) suggested a New Age definition of spirituality for a New Age workforce. Elmes and Smith proposed that empowerment of the New Age worker supported the belief that work was not just a job but also a calling. Empowerment enables the workers to grasp reasons that work is important, ideal, and a process of self-management consistent with New Age beliefs. Scharmer (2009) proposed the emergence of a new spirituality that defines an individual's source of creativity. However, Scharmer insisted that spirituality was distinct from religion and concerns experience rather than specific belief systems.

Mohamed, Wisnieski, Askar, and Syed (1993) reported confusion, frustration, and a lack of clarity regarding multiple definitions and perspectives regarding spirituality. Mohamed et al. conclude that multiple definitions were more complementary rather than mutually exclusive because each focused on an essential part of spirituality. The distinction between religion and spirituality is unnecessary and artificial (Mohamed et al., 1993).

Major world religions involve a spiritual dimension. Religious services involve spiritual practices such as prayer and meditation. Religious practices such as prayer and fasting may be private individual or group activities whereas yoga and meditation are currently public expressions of spirituality. Persons may err in attempts to generalize religion as negative and spirituality as positive. Legal differentiation of religion versus spirituality would prove to be a significant challenge (Cash, Gray & Rood, 2000). According to Mohamed et al. (1993), "Spirituality appears to be a multi-dimensional phenomenon" with the growing spiritual phenomenon as spiritual leadership (p. 103).

Spiritual Leadership

Karakas (2007) emphasized a paradigm shift for leadership considering increasing uncertainty and chaos in the global community. Karakas suggested that succeeding under the conditions would require changes in "how leaders lead" (p. 44). The author framed spiritual leaders as spiritual visionaries who are "individuals who interpret the universe and people's roles within it" (Karakas, 2007, p. 44). Karakas further articulated:

> Spiritual visionaries articulate with authority, eloquence, and depth of insight. They provide deeper meanings, inspiration, and fresh insights about the human condition. They create and utilize powerful visions, metaphors, and symbols. They are the gateways for humanity to explore new facets of the future, to explore collective consciousness. They pioneer new, dynamic, and flexible ways of thinking about holistic problems and questions about the world. They embody and model the search for wholeness, unity, completeness, love, and fulfillment. (p. 46)

Korac-Kakabadse et al. (2002) described a spiritual leadership approach connected to Eastern philosophies of Taoism and Confucianism. Each Eastern philosophy stresses an approach consistent with individual and social harmony, simplicity, wisdom, discernment, and self-reflection (Korac-Kakabadse et al., 2002). Fry (2003) introduced the purpose of spiritual leadership, "to create vision and value congruence across the strategic, empowered team, and individual levels and ultimately, to foster higher levels of organizational commitment and productivity" (p. 1). Spiritual leadership is also multi-dimensional, requiring visionaries with combinations of spiritual philosophies dedicated to purpose and fostering high levels of individual and organizational commitment (Fry, 2008). However, managing contemporary businesses presents ongoing challenges as organizational leaders and managers attempt to apply best practices to ongoing growth and production occurring daily. The mega-church offers an opportunity to examine spiritual leadership in organizations dedicated to spiritual business.

Mega-Church Organization

Protestant congregations consisting of 2000 or more adults and children attending a routine weekend service define the mega-church (Thumma & Bird, 2008). The focus is on attendance and not membership for mega-church congregations. According to Thumma and Bird (2008), attendance at mega-churches remained consistent for the past eight years while continuing to grow in size as well as lead in multi-ethnic populations, contemporary worship, and minimal involvement in politics. As organizations representing transition, mega-churches offer more worship services by expanding into various locations in the community. Community service becomes more of a priority as the use of radio and television decreases and the role of small groups receives greater emphasis (Thumma & Bird, 2008). After a summary of theoretical perspectives, it is important to define essential terms within the current study.

Definition of Terms

Terms used repeatedly throughout this research study are defined in this section. Additional clarification is important to assist readers of this research.

Authentic Leadership

An integration of evolving leadership constructs, ethics, and positive organizational behavior in professional organizations, research, and scholarly literature contributed to the emergence of an authentic leadership theory (Avolio & Gardner, 2005; Avolio & Luthans, 2006a; Cooper & Nelson, 2006; George, 2003; George, Sims, McLean, & Mayer, 2007; Walumbwa, Avolio, Gardner, Wernsing, & Peterson, 2008). Luthans and Avolio (2003) provided the initial definition for authentic leadership "as a process that draws from both positive and psychological capacities and a highly developed organizational context, which results in both greater self-awareness and self-regulated positive behaviors on the part of leaders and associates, fostering positive self-development" (p. 243). Suggested in increasing evidence in professional and scholarly literature was that an authentic approach to leading was more desirable and effective for advancing personal and professional relationship capacity while achieving significant outcomes in organizations (Avolio, 2005; Avolio & Luthans, 2006b; George et al., 2007).

Diverse themes of authentic leadership are increasing in corporate executive, senior management and front-line manager development programs (Wong & Cummings, 2009). Greater expectations for personal commitment and improvement in working relationships have become the direct link to quality leadership (Wong & Cummings, 2009). Recognition of another leadership phenomenon emerges with the realm of mega-church organizations that deserves attention along with authentic leadership.

Mega-Church

Thumma (2008) is a faculty associate at the Hartford Institute for Religion Research, who conducted the most extensive research regarding the mega-church phenomenon. As of 2008, researchers found approximately 1,200 mega-churches in a national study (Thumma & Bird, 2008). Thumma (2008) suggested mega-churches were also mega-businesses in which pastors appeared as chief executives using business tactics to grow the congregations. An entrepreneurial approach contributes to the explosive growth of mega-churches. Thumma and Bird (2008) extended the description of mega-churches as organizations in transition. Mega-churches offer more worship services in multiple locations (Thumma & Bird, 2008). Significant trends within the past eight years identified were increasing roles of the mega-churches in community service and small groups while decreasing use of radio and television (Thumma & Bird, 2008). In the United States, Lakewood Church, Willow Creek, Saddleback, New Birth, The Potter's House, and World Changers are representative of mega-churches (Thumma & Bird, 2008). Thumma suggested that growth equaled success in the United.States society.

Spiritual leadership is multi-dimensional, requiring visionaries with combinations of spiritual philosophies dedicated to purpose and fostering high levels of individual and organizational commitment (Fry, 2003; Karakas, 2007; Korac-Kakabadse et al., 2002).

Spirituality

"Spirituality is a multi dimensional phenomenon" that encompasses religious and spiritual practices from diverse eastern and western perspectives (Mohamed et al., 1993, p. 103). Major world religions involve a spiritual dimension. Religious services involve spiritual practices such as prayer and meditation. Religious practices such as prayer and fasting may be private individual or group activities whereas yoga and meditation are public expressions of spirituality. Persons may err in attempts to generalize religion as negative and spirituality as positive. The definition of spirituality for this study will not distinguish it from religious practices.

Assumptions

The foundation for the study consisted of multiple inherent assumptions. According to Creswell & Plano-Clark (2007) assumptions assist in directing data collection and analysis. An initial assumption is that there is a primary definition of spirituality. Korac-Kakabadse et al. (2002) suggested a loose definition of spirituality in the literature that appeared to be multi-dimensional while incorporating various philosophies, individual, and group, religious, and spiritual practices. A second assumption was that the mega-church structure consisted of spiritual leaders. Mega-church organizations may include authentic, charismatic, transformational, or even transactional leaders. A third assumption concerns growth and profit in an environment where spiritual leadership exists. Additional research may determine if the existing leadership structure reflects more of the characteristics of authentic leaders rather than spiritual leaders. A fourth assumption was that participants in the study responded honestly to each question in the survey instrument.

Scope and Limitations

The scope of this study was restricted to use of the Spiritual Leadership Survey and Authentic Leadership Questionnaire. The research was restricted to mega-churches within the State of Texas and volunteers participating in mega-church organizations. However, aspects of the study existed that could not be controlled effectively or completely by the researcher. Mega-churches exist globally; however, the study was limited to Christian mega-churches located in the United States. Additional limitations involved only volunteers in Houston, Texas because access to full-time employees were denied to this researcher by all non-denominational mega-church organizations in Houston, Texas.. Second, the study was limited to participants who volunteered to complete all required parts of each research instrument. Finally, only a valid and reliable spiritual leadership and authentic leadership survey was included to determine similarities and differences among leadership constructs. However, the researcher could not control that the participants provided honest responses to survey questions.

Delimitations

According to Lunenburg & Irby (2008) delimitations consist of boundaries. Delimitations may be considered the boundaries that establish limits in a research study. This study was limited to survey instruments related to spiritual and authentic leadership. The participants for this study were restricted to volunteers at mega-church organizations located in Houston, Texas. Full-time and part-time employees were not included in the study because permission was denied to the researcher by mega-church staff.

Summary

The current crisis in leadership has resulted in loss of trust, faith, and respect in diverse disciplines across the United States (Cashman, 2008). Wong and Cummings (2009) concluded that authentic leadership resulting in sustainability included focus on relationships, foundation of morals and ethics, link to positive psychological capital, work engagement, and leader, and follower development. The general topic of the proposed research was to determine if the same or different constructs were measured by using the Spiritual Leadership Survey and the Authentic Leadership Survey using a selection of volunteers in mega-church organizations in Houston, Texas.

Chapter 1 opened with a discussion of the background of the current leadership crisis in the United States including a brief explanation of the specific problem to be studied. A brief statement of the purpose of the dissertation was followed by a discussion of the academic and social significance of the research study, selection of procedures, theoretical perspectives to be used in interpreting findings, definition of terms, assumptions, and determination of scope and limitations.

Chapter 2 provided a review of the current literature regarding the paradigm shift among leadership models, evolution of leadership including rational, natural, and open perspectives, history of spiritual leadership, authentic leadership and mega-church organizations. Controversies in the literature regarding spiritual leadership was followed by a review of recent attempts to suggest how spiritual leadership is one of the most viable alternatives to address the leadership crisis.

CHAPTER 2

Review of the Literature

Chapter 1 provided an introduction to the literature regarding the growing crisis in leadership. Memories of Enron, Arthur Anderson, and Worldcom Incorporated continue to exemplify unethical leadership, social irresponsibility, corruption, and selfish greed. Nevertheless, a new alternative in the form of spiritual leadership philosophy and practice expands into diverse disciplines including business and education (Rojas, 2002). Discussions within this literature review continue the exploration of the evolution of spiritual leadership theory and practice and the possibility of a paradigm shift from previous organizational models. Additional discussions focus on the growing spiritual phenomenon in the workplace and assessment of the mega-church organization as a model of doing business in America. A survey of the literature, research, and historical overview will present past and current discoveries that contribute to a balanced discussion of this new age of spiritual leadership and awareness.

Title Searches, Articles, Research Documents, and Journals

Exploration of the literature and research regarding spiritual leadership continues to indicate significant growth. In comparison, information regarding mega-churches appears smaller in number. At the time of this brief survey involving multiple national bookstore chains, an average of 281 titles on spiritual leadership were listed whereas titles on mega-churches indicated an average of 10. An important finding shows a larger number of titles associating spiritual leadership with work, business, and organizations. Authors correlating spiritual leadership with business, organizations, or work related issues include the following: Vaill (2000); Biberman and Whitty (2000); Bolman and Deal (2001); Ashar and Lane-Maher (2004); Cisikszentmihalyi (2003); Grant, O'Neil, and Stephens (2004); Benefiel (2005); Fry, Matherly, and Vitucci (2005); Fry, Nisieiwcz, Vitucci, and Cedillo (2007); Pandey and Gupta, (2008); Fry and Slocum (2008); Yukl (2009); and Holloway and Moss (2010).

Internet Resources and Websites

The internet offers an abundance of resources for gathering and exploring information regarding spiritual leadership and mega-church organizations. A sample of online internet resources reveals numerous websites associated with spiritual leadership and mega-churches. Specific mega-churches maintain websites associated with their organizations such as Lakewood Church and The Potter's House. Keywords entered in the Google search engine yielded 1,760,000 related websites for spiritual leadership whereas 869,000 related websites were associated with mega-churches. Specific organizations offered services related to spiritual leadership research, professional speakers, or consultation services. The International Institute for Spiritual Leadership and The Robert K. Greenleaf Center are examples of organizations dedicated to an emphasis on spiritual leadership in diverse disciplines. The Hartford Institute for Religion Research contains the most recent and extensive research regarding mega-churches in the nation (Thumma, 2001). However, credibility, and reliability of internet sources is a concern for any scholarly study. Websites refer to spiritual leadership and mega-churches regarding experts in the field, scholarly research, reliability, and specific limitations as valuable information.

Article and Scholarly Research Databases

Scholarly articles related to spiritual leadership and application within diverse organizations have been published by Hicks (2002); Fry (2003); Benefiel (2005); Dent, Higgins, and Wharff (2005); and Fry and Slocum (2008). Surveys of the EBSCOHost database indicated 292 scholarly articles while 25 scholarly journals including peer reviewed were listed in the Proquest database. Gale Power Search results revealed 35 academic journals and 13 books involving spiritual leadership. Relevant doctoral dissertations included research applying spiritual leadership to more diverse disciplines including executive leaders, Geaney (2004); elementary principals, Levy (2000); hospitals, Laing (2005); business executives, Quinnine (2007); public school superintendents, Smith (2007); Moroccan business, Al Arkoubi (2008); team development, Bryan (2009); and residential schools, Jimenez (2010). In addition, reviews of three online databases, EBSCOHost, Proquest and Gale Power Search, using keywords, *spiritual leadership, spiritual leadership, and the United States, mega-church, mega-church and United States, and mega-churches and United States* revealed a total of 2,569 journal articles, book reviews, dissertations, and theses, and popular articles unadjusted for redundancies between databases. Considering the increasing amount of scholarly research and titles in a variety of professional literature from 2000 to 2010, from this keyword search, spiritual leadership and mega-church topics are significant subject areas. Therefore, it is appropriate to continue discussion of the possibility of a paradigm shift among models of leadership.

Historical Overview of the Paradigm Shift

Scott and Davis (2007) suggest a paradigm shift among organizational models while Fry (2003 & 2005) and Fry and Slocum (2008) note a shift regarding models of leadership. Levy (2000) documents experiences regarding executive leadership and spirituality. A business model describes the value a company offers to its customers, network of partners, and stakeholders. Reassessment of older business models provides opportunities to emphasize ethical leadership while supporting employee well-being, sustainability, and social responsibility "without sacrificing profitability, revenue, growth and other indicators of financial solvency and performance" (Fry & Slocum, 2008, p. 88). During developments of organizational systems, a scientific revolution has resulted in multiple paradigms offering "new ways" of understanding old things about organizational structures (Scott & Davis, 2007).

Thomas Kuhn (1996) defines a paradigm as "an accepted model or pattern . . . an object for further articulation and specification under new or more stringent conditions . . . models more successful than their competitors in solving a few problems that the group of practitioners has come to recognize as acute" (p. 23). Kuhn suggests that new paradigms evolve from previous ones, and prior terms and concepts are re-invented to "fall into new relationships." Organizations and issues of relationships involve complex interactions occurring within a system. "Each of these organizational elements—environment, strategy and goals, work and technology, formal organization, informal organization, and people—represents an important component of all organizations" (Scott & Davis, 2007, p. 24).

The 1960s to the 1990s introduced a wide range of competing models or paradigms for studying and testing organizations. The history of theoretical paradigms anchors understanding and interpretations of the changing contours of organizations (Scott & Davis, 2007). Three predominant paradigms—rational systems, natural systems, and open systems—emerged to address the impact and importance of organizational structures and behaviors.

Other perspectives include contingency theory, socio-technical systems, organizational ecology, and network approaches. The unique languages of each paradigm appear to suggest application to all organizations or most conditions (Scott & Davis, 2007). However, review of major organizational paradigms indicates interdependence during subsequent evolution allowing openings for the birth of new paradigms including spiritual leadership (Scott &Davis, 2007). Kuhn (1996) advises that embracing a new paradigm defies evidence provided by problem-solving. Knowing that older paradigms have failed with a few and the new paradigm will succeed, despite a multitude of problems that confront it, is a decision made on faith (p. 158).

The growing spiritual phenomenon in corporate America supports an opening for the birth of a new paradigm (Ashmos & Duchon, 2000). Biberman and Whitty (2000) propose that an increasing number of organizations and their workers are expected to shift to the new spiritual paradigm in the future. However, applications of organizational paradigms are also reflections of systematic perspectives providing insights into organizational practices, goals, strategies, and people. Additional brief discussion of rational, natural and open system perspectives is necessary to explore the evolution of a new spiritual paradigm.

The Rational System Perspective

The rational system "established organizations as a distinctive field of study and is considered the dominant perspective that guides the work of organizational scholars and real-world managers" (Scott & Davis, 2007, p. 28). The first step in building a multi-paradigm of faith begins with the rational system perspective. This perspective timeframe begins in the early twentieth century and extends to the 1960s.

According to Scott and Davis (2007) "rational system theorists stress goal specificity and formalization because each of these elements makes an important contribution to the rationality of organizational action" (p. 36). Emphasis is directed toward control and determination of behavior by different subsets of participants using unobtrusive or more obvious measures. "Control is the most significant means of channeling and coordinating behavior to achieve specified goals" (Scott& Davis, 2007, pp. 57-58). Standardization and formalizing routines are key characteristics of the rational perspective. However, the natural system perspective suggests a more significant connection to human relationships.

The Natural System Perspective

Mayo and the Human Relations School, Barnard's Cooperative System, Selznick's institutional approach, Parson's AGIL schema, and the social conflict model are schools of thought within the natural model tradition (Scott & Davis, 2007). The natural system's approach builds upon the rational system's approach by extending beyond structured programs to connecting with the needs of people. Scott and Davis (2007) suggest that the natural system perspective targets social groups "attempting to adapt and survive in their particular circumstances" (p. 60). Natural system analysts emphasize the need to recognize that, within internal, organizational structures, the participants' intelligence and initiative are the most valuable resources. Other natural system perspectives provide various insights regarding the "survival" of social systems and organizational cultures that also appear to relate to issues of the growing spiritual phenomenon in the workplace. Bernard's Cooperative System addresses recognition of how "purpose" is a "motivating power" along with the existence of organizational forces more powerful than purpose. The ability to survive, adapt and, innovate despite significant environmental challenges describes Parson's AGIL schema as a third type of natural system perspective.

Parson's AGIL schema details the following needs that must be met for a social system to survive, including "adaptation (the problem of acquiring sufficient resources), goal attainment (the problem of setting and implementing goals), integration (the problem of maintaining solidarity), and latency (the problem of creating, preserving and transmitting the system's distinctive culture and values)" (Scott & Davis, 2007, p. 77). The AGIL schema may be compared to the internal systems approach that also focuses on adaptation and innovation for organizational system survival. Hesselbein, Goldsmith, andBeckhard (2000) strongly suggest that, although business performance is a good objective, a company must also be agile and able to sustain multiple changes. Organizational design and change have a significant impact upon performance and effectiveness. According to Jones (2004), one of the challenges to evaluating effectiveness within an organization is to use an "internal systems approach." This approach requires an organization to "creatively coordinate resources with employee skills to innovate products and adapt to changing customer needs" (p. 53). Evaluation of mega-churches, later in this discussion, provides insights regarding an internal systems approach that contributes to continued growth and profitability of this alternative model in leadership and business management. However, this discussion must include the open systems approach as part of the evolution toward the new paradigm shift.

The Open System Perspective

Key characteristics of the open system are variety, diversity, and consideration of the environment. People, resources, and information from internal and external sources are other significant parts of the open system perspective. Still, a major component of open systems is the fluidity of joining and engaging inside and outside of the existing organization. Cashman (2008) is an avid proponent of "leading from the inside out" (p. 1). "Much of the work in open systems is around the connections and affective ties that hold these systems together" (Scott & Davis, 2007, p. 3). Suggestions of paradigm shifts in leadership and traditional organizational models would support the open system perspective. Within the following summary of key characteristics of the open systems perspective, Scott and Davis (2007) provide additional connection to growth of the spiritual phenomenon in corporate America. The emphasis upon meaning is a significant part of the spiritual movement. Within an open systems environment organizations create meaning during the adaptation process. Efforts to create meaningful interactions are in agreement with open systems scholars more concerned about the process and activities that meet the needs of diverse and complex systems.

Scharmer (2009) proposes the emergence of a new spirituality with spiritual intelligence that will enhance the ability to access authentic purpose and self. Challenges to spiritual poverty provide spiritual leaders with opportunities to redefine personal and professional values while encouraging reconnection to meaningful purpose in diverse organizational environments (Scharmer, 2009). Organizational leaders continue to urge organizations to increase emphasis on spirituality and spiritual values (Bolman & Deal, 2001). Executives and managers have discovered meditations and spiritual practices to define meaning in their roles and cope with stressful expectations in their work environments (Dehler & Welsh, 1994). Current research regarding spirituality reflects diverse disciplines including psychology, sociology, and health (Rojas, 2002). The movement toward the fourth wave and spiritually based firms is occurring in theory and practice despite lack of universal recognition as the wave of the future (Wagner-Marsh & Conley, 1999).

A current, rational system in corporate America, focusing on rules and order, opens toward the possibilities of a spiritual movement consisting of meaning, purpose, and a sense of community (Ashmos & Duchon, 2000). New approaches to spirituality are increasing in importance to postmodern workers seeking inspiration, meaning, and significance in their work (Elmes & Smith, 2001; Dehler & Welsh, 1994; Kinjerski & Skrypnek, 2008). An emerging perception connects spirituality and leadership as a measure of success in a community, business, or organization (Magnusen, 2002). Combinations of individual spirit and organizational spirit at work result in positive outcomes for individual employees and employers (Kinjerski & Skrypnek, 2008). Research conducted regarding spirituality and job behavior proposes that "strong spiritual factors in a person's personality results in increased tolerance of work failure, decreased susceptibility to stress, favor toward a democratic style of leadership, increased trust, higher tolerance of human diversity, exhibition of altruistic and citizenship behavior, more commitment to the organization and work group increases" (Mohamed et al., 1993, p. 105). This research proposes that in an age of uncertainty, the 21st century requires a spiritual leader and visionary who paves the way toward a paradigm shift in leadership growth and change. Along with the paradigm shift in leadership are significant transformations in organizational design. Mega-churches represent the new corporate structure indicating a paradigm shift in leadership strategies, management techniques, and technological trends.

Mega-churches are the social phenomenon in American society with significant growth occurring within the past 30 years. Mega-church success appears to combine spirituality and effective management in the organizational structure to lead old business and leadership models into the new age. A review of the literature investigates spirituality in the workplace, spiritual leadership and the mega-church phenomenon as interrelated parts of re-defining the meaning of work in America. However, authentic leadership also emerges as a significant force adding to the cry for greater honesty, ethical commitment and moral development among leaders in the global community.

Demonstrating Authentic Leadership

Distress and disappointment in leadership within social, political, economic, educational, health, and business arenas supports the need for genuine change (Shirey, 2006). "Highly publicized corporate scandals, management malfeasance, and broader societal challenges, facing public and private organizations contributes to the recent focus on authenticity and authentic leadership" (Walumbwa et al., 2008, p. 90).

Authentic Leadership Development reveals significant differences from current leadership theories, suggesting that authentic leadership represents a root construct. Therefore, authentic leadership would be a root construct of positive leadership and the foundation for similar leadership theories related to positive psychology. Consequently, differentiating between authentic and similar leadership perspectives becomes important to building a theory of authentic leadership and developing support for conceptual independence in addition to a case for construct validation (Avolio & Gardner, 2005).

A leader exemplifying genuine morals, character, and integrity with the ability to grow and sustain people in the organization reveals authentic competency (Storr, 2004; Sarros & Cooper, 2006). Avolio & Gardner (2005) support a shift in leadership focus to increasing awareness of the leader's relationship with self and significant others in an organization. Profound interest in authentic leadership is evident in applied literature (George, Sims, McLean, & Mayer, 2007; George & Sims, 2007) and academic management literature (Avolio & Luthans, 2006a; Avolio & Walumbwa, 2006). However, Cooper, Scandura, and Schriesheim (2005) as well as Walumba et al. (2008), propose an even higher order, multidimensional construct of authentic leadership including traits, behaviors, contexts, individual, and team organization.

According to Garger (2008), authentic leadership involves the delivery of leadership behaviors rather than what composes the leadership behavior. Leaders demonstrating authentic behavior focus on self-awareness and relational transparency while inspiring and motivating followers to engage in the same process. According to Cummings, Hayduk, and Estabrooks (2005), leaders in the nursing discipline who demonstrated positive relational orientations diminished emotional exhaustion among nurses, resulting in increased job satisfaction and supervision. Considering the essential behaviors demonstrated by authentic leaders, Walumba et al. (2008) summarize four components of authentic leadership in an Authentic Leadership Questionnaire (ALQ) including self-awareness, relational transparency, balanced processing, and internalized moral perspective. Authentic leadership is a significant alternative for transforming the workplace. However, attention is also upon spirituality at work and reframing meaning for workers in the new millennium.

Spirituality in the Workplace

Transformations in the workplace are a response to the changing nature of work (Pawar, 2008). Chakraborty and Chakraborty (2004) suggest a growing interest in workplace spirituality, management, and the spirit of a transformational leader. A new item appearing on conference agendas is evidence of increasing interest for spirituality in the workplace. Fry, Nisieiwcz, Vitucci, andCedillo (2007) presented *Transforming City Government Through Spiritual Leadership* at the National Academy of Management; Fry, Nisieiwcz, andVitucci (2007) presented *Transforming Police Organizations Through Spiritual Leadership* at the National Academy of Management; Fry and Matherly (2006) presented *Spiritual Leadership as an Integrating Paradigm for Positive Leadership* at the Gallup International Leadership Summit; Fry and Matherly (2006) presented *Spiritual Leadership and Organizational Performance* at the National Academy of Management; Fry and Whittington (2005) presented *Spiritual Leadership Theoryas a Paradigm for Organizational Development* at the National Academy of Management; and Malone and Fry (2003) presented *Transforming Schools Through Spiritual Leadership: A Field Experiment* at the 2003 National Academy of Management.

Spiritual lessons are incorporated into the organizational environments of successful and diverse companies including Taco Bell, Pizza Hut, BioGenenex, Aetna International, Big Six Accounting's Deloitte and Touche, and law firms like New York's Kaye, Scholar, Fierman, Hays and, Haroller (International Institute for Spiritual Leadership, 2010). Increasing numbers of leaders, managers, and executives are incorporating spiritual practices in their personal and professional lives (Milliman, 2008; Cavanagh, Hanson, Hanson, & Hinojoso, 2004). Popular and scholarly literature indicates significant growth in the number of articles and books regarding workplace spirituality (Mitroff & Denton, 1999; Delbecq, 1999; Ashmos & Duchon, 2000; Howard, 2002; Klenke, 2005; Kinjerski & Skrypnek, 2004; Fry & Whittington, 2005; Fry & Matherly, 2006). Incorporating spirituality into management theory, development, and practice is included in growing amounts of research and literature (Cacioppe, 2000a; Cacioppe, 2000b). Heaton et al. (2004) highlight the emergence of new management, spirituality, and religion interest group in the Academy of Management.

Brandt (1996) suggests that "The search for spirituality and interest in integrating spirituality with everyday work life gained momentum during the late 1990s" (p. 49). The spiritual journey at work began quietly without revealing discontent or challenging the existing organizational structure or environment (Burack, 1999). Later, the quiet journey became a movement as Baby Boomers approached middle age, questioning purpose in life and assessing quality of accomplishments.

Downsizing trends, demand for additional hours at work, advancing information technology, and increasing stress triggered reflections of loss of security for the American worker. Cavanaugh, Hanson, Hanson, and Hinojoso (2001) propose that the workplace has become the place to express one's spirituality in the context of empowerment and personal growth. "Workers spend more time and emotional energy in the workplace than in any other place or segment of their lives . . . for many the workplace becomes a substitute for family and friends as a source of emotional connectivity and meaning" (p. 45). The year 2000 signified the start of a new millennium and additional reflections from workers about new commitments for the future, interesting and, meaningful work, connection, and positive social relationships, and lives that do not conflict with defining themselves as human beings (Pfeffer, 2003; Duchon & Plowman, 2005).

Throughout the literature, a recurring theme indicates that people want a connection between spirituality and work to seek values beyond just earning a paycheck (Klenke, 2005). "Working people and human evolution itself are constantly seeking meaning, purpose and a sense of contribution to work-life. These needs are best served and deepened when a spiritual paradigm frames the intentions of all stakeholders" (Biberman & Whitty, 1997, p. 135). Dehler and Welsh (1994) propose an emerging organizational transformation described as a "new management paradigm." Within the new paradigm is a challenge for prior traditional, rational, and scientific management approaches. Organizational spirituality is the paradigm shift toward the genesis of spiritual leadership that continues significant transformations into the new age world of work.

Historical Trends for Spiritual Leadership

In the 1940s and 1950s, effective leadership was connected to productivity and profit while the social structure in the United States began significant changes. Leaders in diverse disciplines including government, business, and religion struggle to maintain some sense of community (Magnusen, 2002). By mid-century United States citizens lost faith in their leaders who became complacent with accomplishments in science and technology while corporate infrastructures broke into multiple fragments. Expectations, after decades of corporate instability, indicated a redefinition of leadership that focused on the value of people, community, andshared vision (Magnusen, 2002).

Covey (2004) suggests that the business world was undergoing a spiritual renaissance. Business leadership in the 21st century became a transformational experience as leaders developed into social artists, spiritual visionaries, and cultural innovators (Karakas, 2007). Biberman and Whitty (1997) describe a major shift from a modern paradigm with "autocratic paternalistic stewardship" and rational, scientific approaches to a spiritual paradigm. However, other researchers suggest since the industrial revolution, dominant organizational structures resembled centralized, standard, bureaucratic systems (Dean, Fornaciari, & Mcgee, 2002; Fry, 2003). Traditional rationality" resides in the structure itself not in individual participants. Emphasis is on control and determination of behavior of one subset of participants by another . . . most rational system theorists view control as channeling and coordinating behavior to achieve specified goals" (Scott &Davis, 2007, pp. 57-58). A spiritual paradigm perspective involves openness to change, a sense of purpose and meaning in life, connection with a greater whole, individual understanding, and expression of one's own spirituality (Fry, 2005).

However, an emerging postmodern management paradigm emphasizes spiritual principles and practices that will serve as the catalyst for transforming existing organizations. Workers and managers are seeking more meaning in their work (Ashar & Lane-Maher, 2004). The flat organization structure that is open and adaptable to change reflects the spiritual paradigm. Workers are empowered at all levels of the company while emphasizing creative thinking and teamwork to develop and execute mutual agreements regarding mission statements and objectives for the organization (Mintzberg et al., 2003). Yet a significant connection exists between spirituality and leadership. Additional explosions have occurred in organizational literature pertaining to spirituality and leadership such as Vaill, 2000; Fairholm, 2001; Korac-Kakabadse et al., 2002; Fry, 2003; Wharff, 2004. Spiritual leadership becomes another essential piece in the paradigm shift of the 21st century.

Spiritual Leadership

The history of spiritual leadership cites Fairholm (1996, 1997, 1998) as the initial scholar who combined the components of spirituality and leadership. He proposed that spiritual leadership was a holistic approach that considers the needs of leaders and followers while it creates an environment that grows and nurtures others. Review of the literature supports this approach by suggesting that "the roots of effective leadership may be grounded in a spiritual dimension" (Klenke, 2005, p. 56). A spiritual leadership approach will,

Add value to an organization by helping workers and managers align personal and organizational values around their understanding of spirituality . . . [it] is beginning to be recognized as important in the overall development of a leader. According to this view, common characteristics of effective leaders are an inward focus, potential for self-discovery, reflective analysis, and personal reinvention. (p. 56)

Spiritual leadership theory has continued evolving among multiple scholars who focus on clarifying both leadership and spiritual components (Fairholm, 1997; Sanders et al., 2003; Fry, 2003; Benefiel, 2005). Hoppe (2005) frames spiritual leadership as "spirit-driven leadership" that requires courage when confronted with difficult decisions and challenges arising from the intellectual and rational being. Cashman (2008) encourages ongoing contemplation for leaders to discover spirituality by determining who they are and what they indeed believe. Sanders et al. (2003) explore the spiritual dimensions of leadership by considering the possibility of an integrated theory that shows a hierarchical relationship between transcendental, transformational, and transactional theories. Fry, Vitucci, and Cedillo (2005) conclude that spiritual leadership offers the potential for a new paradigm for leadership theory, research and practice given that it "incorporates and extends transformational and charismatic theories as well as ethics and values-based theories (e.g. authentic and servant leadership); and avoids the pitfalls of measurement model misspecification" (p. 1). Fry (2003) continues to elaborate on defining spiritual leadership as "the values, attitudes, and behaviors necessary to intrinsically motivate one's self and others so that they have a sense of spiritual survival through calling and membership" (p. 838). Fry (2005) expands spiritual leadership theory to address positive human health and wellbeing considering further developments in workplace spirituality, spiritual leadership, and character ethics. Fry, Matherly, and Vittuci (2005) emphasize how "spiritual leadership theory is an emerging paradigm for organization development and transformation that draws from positive organizational scholarship." Spiritual leadership "creates a vision wherein leaders and followers experience a sense of calling in that their life has meaning and makes a difference; establishes a social/organizational culture based on the values of altruistic love whereby leaders and followers have a sense of membership, feel understood and appreciated, and have genuine care, concern and appreciation for both self and others" (p. 338).

The spiritual leadership challenge appears to be a struggle for balance to demonstrate performance management as a rational approach and a sense of meaning or purpose as a spiritual approach. Milliman (2008) questions how spiritual leadership manifests in practice. Portions of the literature provide examples of the impact of Christian leadership on executive leadership behavior (Delbecq, 1999); applications of spiritual leadership characteristics by business leaders (Fry & Slocum, 2008); and a case study of an entrepreneur (Milliman, 2008). Collins and Porras (2002) conducted longitudinal research on 18 "visionary" companies considered leaders in their industries, exceeding 50 years with results indicating that each company's success is because of a focus on core values based on non-economic beliefs and empowering cultures. Results from the longitudinal study also reveal the visionary performance during long terms with no focus on maximizing profits.

Prior research performed by Peters and Waterman (1982) using "excellent" companies resulted in similar results. Successful companies continue to be the focus of research regarding how spiritual practices and leadership are incorporated into the organizational structure. Recent research by Fry, Vitucci & Cedillo, (2005) tested spiritual leadership theory and Army transformation resulting in strong support for positive relationships and qualities of the spiritual leadership model. Spiritual leadership in practice is creating large amounts of discussion for leaders seeking the path from theory to application. Southwest Airlines and Starbucks are two successful organizations that prompted investigations of incorporating spirituality in the workplace.

Spiritual Leadership in Practice

Millimann (2008) acknowledges the increased interest for spirituality in business. Fry and Slocum (2008) report that Chik-fil-A and Interstate Batteries were companies with strong spiritual foundations and practices. Research supports a paradigm shift at the Chief Executive Officer level, creating an opening for building spiritual principles into organizational structures. As a case study of Southwest Airlines exemplifies, "spiritual-based values [guide] its organizational goals and practices and . . . [establish] a track record of excellent organizational performance as well as high employer and customer satisfaction" (Milliman et al., 1999, p. 222). The authors examined how Southwest Airlines manifested spirituality in its organization and assessed the impact on employees, customers, and organizational performance. Southwest Airlines' spiritual values include a sense of cause by providing low airfares and personable service. Moreover, the organization acts as a community; it encourages feelings of making a difference; failures are treated as opportunities for growth; teamwork and serving others are defined as acting in the best interests of the company; empowerment and commitment to a strong work ethic benefit employees and the organization. Three propositions form these primary results from the research. The first proposition suggests that company spiritual values that address both mental and emotional aspects of employees instead of just "pay" will have a positive impact on employee work attitudes, spiritual attitudes, and organizational performance (p. 230). The second proposition advises that empowering employees with input regarding company decisions results in experiences of stronger connections to company spiritual values, employee spiritual attitudes, and organizational performance. The third proposition recommends alignment of human resource management practices with company spiritual values to create a positive link to stronger employee attitudes and organizational performance.

One other company shares the honor of practicing spirit at work. Marques (2008) finds that "spiritual behavior at the organizational level does lead to enhanced corporate performance; workplace spirituality, when encouraged by top management, is oftentimes instigated by personal life experiences, and spiritual behavior, at the organizational level, leads to advantages by multiple stakeholders" (p. 248). The researcher assessed organizational performance for the Starbucks Corporation by using the definition of workplace spirituality as a guiding principle. Results of the research study indicate that as a leader in the industry, the Starbucks Corporation exhibits interconnectedness; authenticity, reciprocity, and personal goodwill; a deep sense of meaning; greater motivation and organizational excellence. The author concludes that spirit at work is not merely a fad when a successful corporation such as Starbucks "represents financial health, guarantees a progressive working environment, demonstrates commitment to innovation and epitomizes corporate social responsibility" (p. 255). Another corporation may join this honorable group to represent spirituality in the workplace, yet research is minimal. Mega-churches are the growing corporations of the new millennium representing spirituality and leadership in the workplace.

Mega-Churches Mega-Corporations

When one considers the expanding practice of spirituality and spiritual leadership in business, curiosity exists regarding the mega-church as a mega-business. Many regard the church as a place of worship, spiritual growth, and illumination; however, the church is also a significant business requiring effective leadership, teamwork, andquality service. Recent studies regarding church growth target the mega-church phenomenon with congregations of at least 2000 or more members and million dollar budgets (Thumma, 2001), yet little or no research exists regarding leadership practices in mega-church management.

According to a survey published by Hartford Institute for Religion Research (2008), size defines mega-churches. The average weekly attendance at mega-churches may include 3,857 persons (Thumma, 2001). Over the past 20 years, attendance at mega-churches increased by an average rate of 90% (Thumma, 2001). A study conducted in 1999 indicates the average total annual income of mega-churches was $4.8 million (Thumma, 2001). Mega-churches resemble corporate structures attempting to address the best leadership practices, management strategies, and technological advances. According to Drucker (1999), mega-churches are the most important social phenomenon in American society within the past 30 years. Drucker suggests that the explosion of mega-churches is a result of re-defining value for the "nonchurchgoer." Success for mega-churches appears to be a combination of focus on spirituality instead of ritual and effective management of servicesDrucker (1999). The mega-church as a mega-corporation deserves study to determine its spiritual leadership practices and to view it as a workplace that appears to have factors contributing to its growth and success. The focus of this study will be three of the largest mega-church organizations in Texas. A brief history of Lakewood Church will exemplify the birth of a mega-church organization.

Brief History of Lakewood Church

On Mother's Day 1959 the first meeting of Lakewood Church was held in an abandoned feed store on the outskirts of Houston, Texas. Founding Pastors John and Dodie Osteen led a diverse, non-denominational congregation. Church expansion included a weekly television program viewed in 100 countries around the world. John Osteen authored 45 books while Dodie Osteen documented her miraculous healing from cancer. John Osteen sponsored conferences and seminars held in Houston and around the world. Prior to John Osteen's death in 1999, his son Joel Osteen established an international reputation in media and business. Joel Osteen attended Oral Roberts University where he studied radio and television communications. Joel returned to Houston in 1982 and not only founded Lakewood's television ministry but also produced John Osteen's television ministry for 17 years until his father's death in 1999.

As a successful television producer, Joel pursued the vision of global outreach and created the John Osteen television program. "The capstone on his career was building KTBU-TV55 into a premier independent television station for the Houston market" (Young, 2006, p. 16). After the unexpected passing of John Osteen, the son Joel became Senior Pastor of Lakewood Church. Community outreach continued to grow as Lakewood's international media broadcasts expanded globally. According to a study regarding mega-churches in Hartford Institute for Religion Research (2008), Lakewood is one of the fastest growing churches in America. July 14, 2005 is a moment in history when the church congregation moved into a $95 million renovated Compaq Center with a 16,000 seat arena and with 38,000 persons attending church services weekly. In 2004 Joel Osteen authored his first book, *Best Life Now,* which remained on the New York Times bestseller list for more than two years and sold more than four million copies. Lakewood Church is history in the making and is the social and spiritual phenomenon of the new millennium (Young, 2006).

Conclusions

Burke (2006) believes that a paradigm shift from traditional, scientific management to spiritual leadership will reveal a hard struggle between rational and meaningful perspectives. The author is critical of attempts to measure spirituality by suggesting that it "implies an 'end' or a 'goal'—for example, 'I am more spiritual than you because my Spirituality 360 degree feedback tells me so'" (p. 19). Burke also indicates that it would be possible for a new leadership paradigm to emerge without a combination of emotional and spiritual Intelligence.

Zohar and Marshall (2004) support defining exceptional leadership by the reflection of "spiritual capital." They emphasize that spiritually intelligent leadership requires a radical change in prior philosophies and practices of leadership in business. Spiritual leadership includes intelligence of the mind, heart, and spirit. They suggest that future research regarding spiritual leadership include spiritual intelligence as an essential piece.

Markow and Klenke (2005) summarize implications for future research regarding spiritual leadership by reporting that it remains a new construct in the early stages of development. The authors describe emerging empirical research as an "important beginning." Recent research by Fry, Vitucci, and Cedillo (2005) provides support for causal relationships between qualities of spiritual leadership and organizational commitment and productivity. Sanders et al. (2003) report a significant causal relationship between leadership, spirituality, and organizational commitment. Van Knippenberg, van Knippenberg, De Cremer, and Hogg (2004) have performed a multi-method study including a laboratory experiment, scenario experiment, and two surveys that resulted in enhanced levels of productivity and effective leadership. However, the authors report that "qualitative methodologies in building a theory of spiritual leadership remain largely unexplored and epistemological and methodological pluralism is needed for future research" (p. 22).

Summary

A new age of spiritual awareness is here. Reviews of the literature provide ample evidence of organizational writers urging increasing attention toward defining spirituality, spiritual values, spirituality in the workplace and spiritual leadership. Executives have discovered spiritual practices to define meaning in their roles and started personal transformations that affected entire organizational structures. Spirituality was no longer merely a personal practice but a means of doing business.

Spirituality at work is a growing phenomenon as workers re-define traditional aspects of work to expand toward an experience with cause, meaning, and purpose. Researchers suggest that the spiritual movement is similar to a fourth wave of the future. Along with waves of change are leaders who face social, economic, and political challenges that transform nations. Alternative leadership models are resulting in new spiritual leadership paradigms bringing forth the new age approach to postmodern workers seeking inspiration, meaning, and significance in their work.

The measure of success is no longer maximizing profit but meaningful management of multiple aspects of life. Spiritual leadership offers the paradigm shift required to expand transformational models and press toward another level of transcendence while mega-churches offer the opportunity to study spiritual leadership practices in a new corporate structure. Two significant social and spiritual phenomena are creating a significant impact in American society. Continued investigation of spirituality in the workplace, spiritual leadership, and the mega-church corporation as interrelated parts is an opportunity to contribute to the spirit at work. Multiple authors propose possible implications to shifting toward a new paradigm of spiritual leadership and spirituality in the workplace.

CHAPTER 3

Method

The results of this dissertation study contributed to the growing body of knowledge regarding spiritual leadership, authentic leadership, and mega-church organizations. The purpose of this quantitative research was to determine if the same or different constructs existed by comparing The Spiritual Leadership Survey and The Authentic Leadership Questionnaire by distributing both instruments among a selection of 100 volunteers located at mega-churches in Houston, Texas.

Chapters one and two presented a thorough review of recent ethical issues in organizations, suggesting spiritual leadership as a growing phenomenon reinventing the nature of business. The current chapter will elaborate on the specific research method and design recommended for this study.

Research Method and Design Appropriateness

The proposal for this study included recommendations for a quantitative research method and correlational research design. The initial stage of the study involved a non-experimental quantitative approach using the Revised Spiritual Leadership Survey and The Authentic Leadership Questionnaire 1.0 rater version. According to The International Institute for Spiritual Leadership (2010), The Spiritual Leadership Survey was one of the most extensively tested assessment tools regarding spirituality in the workplace. Results of the study determined if The Spiritual Leadership Survey was measuring the same or different constructs than The Authentic Leadership Questionnaire. Additional variables included age, gender, occupation, income, and racial/ethnic group. This study used a selection of 100 volunteers who comprised the survey population. However, additional discussions also included the appropriateness of a quantitative method and correlational research design. The research problem determined the appropriateness of the research design.

The Quantitative Method

Quantitative research is one of the most common methodologies used in human and social sciences (Cooper & Schindler, 2008). Activities associated with a quantitative approach include an attempt by the researcher to describe, sample, compare, or evaluate (Cooper & Schindler, 2008). Research problems that involve describing trends or explaining the relationship among variables is a part of the quantitative approach (Creswell, 2009). Additional characteristics of the quantitative method involves addressing specific questions, identifying independent and dependent variables, collecting numerical data from research participants, analyzing numeric data using statistics, and reporting results without bias (Creswell, 2009). The quantitative method describes a problem that provides an explanation by obtaining an estimate or sample of a population. Reviewing the literature provides the means for discovering multiple variables and using statistical techniques to determine an association between chosen variables (Cooper & Schindler, 2008).

Qualitative research involves an analysis of data based on themes or similar characteristics. Tools with content analysis capabilities would search for common themes and similar characteristics regarding text, phrases, people or events. However, a different tool for quantitative research requires statistical analysis, manipulation of numerical data and performance of various computations that determine if relationships exist between variables. The Statistical Package for Social Sciences, or SPSS, is an example of a tool for quantitative research with the ability to perform complex statistical analysis, computations, and graphical displays of numerical data. Robert Robinson, Ph.D. is considered an expert in statistical procedures. Dr. Robinson offers current knowledge and experience from teaching college level statistics courses and active consulting as an industrial organizational psychologist. Dr. Robinson performed ongoing consultation regarding the method and design of this study.

The quantitative method was appropriate for this research study because it provided an opportunity to explain any possible associations among constructs considered part of The Spiritual Leadership Survey and The Authentic Leadership Questionnaire. The research design provided a blueprint for main objectives to answer essential questions (Cooper & Schindler, 2008). A correlational design was the optimum choice for this specific research to accomplish the goals for this study. "Correlational designs are procedures in quantitative research in which investigators measure the degree of association (or relationship) between two or more variables using the statistical procedure of correlational analysis" (Creswell, 2005, p. 18). Attempts to control or manipulate variables do not occur in correlational research designs because variables are observed as they exist naturally in the environment (Gravetter & Wallnau, 2005). The correlational research design included specific statistical tests that determined if a relationship existed among constructs in the Spiritual Leadership Survey and Authentic Leadership Questionnaire.

Qualitative Research Designs

Creswell (2009) also mentions multiple qualitative research designs not appropriate for this study, including grounded theory, ethnographic or narrative. Qualitative research is a recent phenomenon, displaying a major role in educational research only within the past 30 years (Creswell, 2009). First, grounded theory designs focus on collecting interview data from people, forming categories and themes, and constructing a figure or visual model that embodies an overall explanation (Creswell, 2009). Second, ethnographic designs describe, analyze, and interpret behavioral patterns, beliefs and language that develop in a particular cultural group or groups over time (Creswell, 2009). Finally, narrative research designs provide an opportunity to collect and tell stories of the lives of individual persons, and write narratives about personal or professional experiences. When one considers descriptions of each qualitative design, the correlational design is more appropriate for this study to explain whether a positive, negative, or no relationship exists among constructs when comparing The Spiritual Leadership Survey and The Authentic Leadership Questionnaire. Qualitative research design procedures do not measure degrees of association between variables or use statistical procedures common in quantitative research studies.

Correlational Research Designs

Correlational research designs express degrees of association between variables as a number that informs the researcher whether two or more variables are related or whether a relationship exists (Creswell, 2009). However, correlation studies are not cause and effect (Simon & Francis, 2004). Results of the correlational study will not determine that spiritual leadership causes organizational growth and profit. However, statistical tests will determine whether the constructs among The Spiritual Leadership Survey and Authentic Leadership Questionnaire are related.

This particular research study will not link quantitative and qualitative research designs as a mixed-method. Numerical data and statistical analysis will be part of the primary quantitative method rather than adding interviews, analysis of text, or images. According to Creswell (2009), action research designs include a mixture of quantitative and qualitative data. Still, the focus of action research designs is the educational environment. Addressing improvements in teaching, the educational environment or student learning suggest use of the action research design. Therefore, the action research design is not appropriate for this study that focuses on mega-church business environments. Nevertheless, a research study is not complete without a research question to guide the study. Quantitative research involves specific, narrow questions with the purpose of obtaining measurable, observable data on a selection of variables (Creswell, 2005).

Research Question

According to Onwuegbuzie and Leach (2005), research questions determine the choice of research methodology. Cooper and Schindler (2005) emphasize additional characteristics of research questions including fact-orientation, using information gathering, and "the hypothesis of choice that best states the objective of the research study" (p. 15). The intent of this quantitative study was to describe the direction and strength of a possible relationship among constructs within The Spiritual Leadership Survey and Authentic Leadership Questionnaire using a selection of volunteers in mega-church organizations in Houston, Texas. Cooper and Schindler (2008) suggest that "hypotheses start with the basic research question that develops specific predictions about the nature of the relationship between the variables identified in the question" (p. 37).

The following research question guided this study:

R1: Does the Spiritual Leadership Survey measure the same or different constructs than The Authentic Leadership Questionnaire for volunteers in mega-churches located in Houston, Texas?

From this research question, the null hypothesis states:

H0: The Spiritual Leadership Survey measures the same constructs as the Authentic Leadership Questionnaire for volunteers in mega-churches located in Houston, Texas.

An alternative hypothesis from the research question states:

H1: The Spiritual Leadership Survey measures different constructs than The Authentic Leadership Questionnaire for volunteers in mega-churches located in Houston, Texas.

Correlational research does not involve controlling the values of variables so there is no independent or dependent variable. Causal relationships are not established in correlational studies. Causal language is more common in experimental and quasi-experimental studies. The terms independent variable, dependent variable or implications of causation were not included in this study because of relationships found in statistical results.

This research study determined the strength of association among variables when comparing The Spiritual Leadership Survey and The Authentic Leadership Questionnaire. However, additional planning of the study involved identifying the target population, and selecting the sample.

Population

The target population included a proposal of which individuals and how many of them would participate in the research study. A sample of the target population, representing a larger group, assisted this researcher in statistical hypothesis testing and estimating population values (Cooper & Schindler, 2008). Characteristics of the population and sample under investigation consisted of 100 volunteers, age 18 and older, currently providing volunteer services in mega-church organizations. Geographical limitations included the city of Houston, Texas to allow convenient access to a large number of participants. According to a survey published by the Hartford Institute for Religion Research (2008), 193 mega-churches currently exist in Texas. A mega-church organization consists of at least 2000 members. However, multiple mega-churches in Houston, Texas exceed 2000 members. The general population focused on mega-churches in Houston, Texas with a minimum of 2000 or greater members. Only volunteers were included in the survey because the roles of full-time and part-time employees are defined differently from volunteers.

Sampling Frame

Valid responses from The Spiritual Leadership Survey and The Authentic Leadership Questionnaire were gathered from a sample of 100 volunteers. The selection criteria consisted of obtaining a sample of males and females, age 18 and older, currently providing services in mega-church organizations with 2000 or greater members. Initial data collection involved use of a non-probability snowball sampling method because requests to administer surveys to the population of full-time employees in the entire population of non-denominational mega-churches located in Houston, Texas were denied to the researcher of this study. The process for selection involved a chain referral process in which one volunteer referred another volunteer willing to participate in the research study. Only volunteers were included in the research study because the roles of full-time and part-time employees are defined differently from volunteers. The sample size was verified using statistical software that also determined the appropriate margin of error and level of confidence. Chain referral data collection continued until an appropriate number of responses were collected. A stratified sample would have been used if demographic information about the sample was not available.

Informed Consent

Each participant was informed, prior to completing each survey that participation was voluntary. Each participant had the opportunity to review and agree to the informed consent form prior to participation in the study. Individuals, who chose not to participate had no additional obligations to provide information for the research study. An introductory cover letter and informed consent form was included in the e-mail sent to all participants describing the intent of the study and request for their cooperation. The e-mail also contained the personal contact number and e-mail address of the researcher. The introductory letter was followed by the informed consent form detailing any potential risks or benefits and withdrawal procedures. Research in this social and behavioral science context did not subject participants to any mental, emotional stressors, physical, social, or psychological risks. Participants were volunteers, providing services in mega-church organizations, who answered survey questions regarding leadership behavior based on their knowledge, observations and service experience. Participants, who had the desire to withdraw after data collection was completed had the option do so in writing by sending an e-mail to the researcher with the alpha-numeric code and short statement requesting withdrawal from the study. The researcher would identify withdrawn participants by adding "W" to the end of the participant's code. Information from withdrawn participants would not be included in analysis of research data or conclusions. If a large number of participants chose to withdraw from a specific mega-church location in Houston, Texas, the researcher had the option of another attempt at data collection with new participants at another mega-church obtained from volunteer referrals.

Confidentiality

The researcher guaranteed confidentiality for participants who responded to surveys in this study. The statement of informed consent addressed all issues pertaining to confidentiality. The confidentiality statement informed participants that they were free to participate, not participate, or withdraw at any time. Anonymity was guaranteed, and participants were informed that individual responses would not be included in the final dissertation or returned to administrative staff in the organization.

Neither the names nor any other identifying information was used for any participant. Individual identity was protected throughout the study by assigning each participant a code. The coding system included a combination of letters and numbers. Each participant was coded by letters MA indicating Mega-Church A and Subject numbers one, two, three or MB indicating Mega-Church B and Subject numbers one, two, three or MC for Mega-Church C Subject numbers one, two, three. Subject numbers continued in sequence until all participants completed surveys within the designated period. The researcher was the only person to have access to the coding procedure.

Individual identities were protected during and after the data collection period because participants were instructed to use his or her participant codes to maintain confidentiality. Data from personal e-mails were stored electronically on the researcher's private computer system in a password protected file. Coding of volunteer participants has been maintained on a password protected computer and in a password protected file to ensure individual confidentiality. Only the researcher has access to the password protected file required to unlock the computer. A second password was required to access the data file. The physical location where the data for the research study has been stored is on the researchers personal, password protected, computer, at the researcher's home. During and after the research study, only the researcher will have access to the researcher's computer at the home location. At the end of the research period all electronic data associated with the study will be disposed of electronically using an erasure file program at the end of three years.

Geographic Location

This study was limited to volunteers currently providing services in mega-church organizations located in the United States. Additional geographic limitations included the city of Houston within the state of Texas. Groups of volunteers at each church selected for involvement in this study had a possibility of receiving a personal visit for addressing any additional questions or issues regarding the electronic administration of each survey.

Data Collection

Electronic data collection methods were used for this study. Volunteers at each mega-church organization were sent an electronic version of the Spiritual Leadership Survey and Authentic Leadership Questionnaire to their personal e-mail address. A random sample of 100 full-time employees could not be obtained because permission to administer surveys was denied to the researcher by every non-denominational mega-church located in the city of Houston, Texas. Demographic data and valid responses from each survey were gathered from a non-probability snowball sample of 100 volunteers at mega-church organizations located in Houston, Texas.

The sample consisted of males and females, age 18 and older, participating as current volunteers in mega-church organizations with 2000 or greater members. Chain referral data selection continued until an appropriate number of participants were selected. Participants were informed, in the cover letter that the average time to complete each survey would be approximately 15 minutes. Participants were allowed five to seven days to return responses to surveys. Only surveys returned within the designated period were considered valid data. Each completed instrument was saved and stored electronically on the researcher's computer at the researcher's home to maintain the integrity of individual responses until data analysis could be performed. The electronic survey method provided greater return rates than traditional surveys by eliminating the need for use of the postal system to return completed surveys. The quantitative data was entered in an SPSS computer program to assist in analysis of the data.

All research data was managed and stored electronically on the researcher's computer with additional password protection. During and after the study, only the researcher will have access to the data stored on the researcher's computer. A password will be required to unlock the researcher's computer while a second password will be required to access any research data. Data at the end of the study will be stored electronically, protected by passwords and destroyed electronically after three years.

Instrumentation

Diverse methods involve collecting data from a group, describing characteristics, opinions, or other aspects of the sample from a population. Fowler (2009) suggests results from surveys describe relationships among variables in addition to comparing groups by using statistical data analysis useful in causal or comparative research designs.

Quantitative research uses predetermined instruments (Creswell, 2009). The Revised Spiritual Leadership Survey and The Authentic Leadership Questionnaire version 1.0 (rater) (Avolio et al. 2007) were the chosen instruments for this research study. The Revised Spiritual Leadership Survey provided a quantitative assessment of the constructs that described spiritual leadership. Permission was granted by Dr. Louis Fry to use The Spiritual Leadership Survey for this research study. The Spiritual Leadership Survey was purchased from The International Spiritual Leadership website. Meanwhile, The Authentic Leadership Questionnaire 1.0 rater version provided quantitative assessment of constructs that comprise authentic leadership. Permission was obtained from Robert Most at Mind Garden, Inc.

Revised Spiritual Leadership Survey

According to The International Institute for Spiritual Leadership (2010), The Spiritual Leadership Survey is one of the most extensively tested assessment surveys regarding workplace spirituality. At least 1200 employees participating in studies including schools, military units, cities, police, and for-profit organizations confirm the reliability and validity of the spiritual leadership model (International Institute for Spiritual Leadership, 2010). The Revised Spiritual Leadership Survey consisted of 18 items. The following nine variables are associated with measuring aspects of spiritual leadership theory: inner life, vision, altruistic love, hope/faith, meaning/calling, membership, life satisfaction, organizational commitment, and productivity. Results from the Spiritual Leadership Survey established a baseline on key spiritual leadership variables and measure levels of organizational success (International Institute for Spiritual Leadership, 2010). 7 scales included in the Spiritual Leadership Survey indicate adequate coefficient alpha reliabilities between .83 and .93 (Fry, 2005).

The Authentic Leadership Questionnaire

The Authentic Leadership Questionnaire 1.0 rater version provided a quantitative assessment of constructs describing authentic leadership regarding self-awareness, transparency, ethical/moral conduct, and balanced processing (Avolio et al. 2007). The rater version of the questionnaire referred to the participant's perception of how frequently each statement fits the leader's particular leadership style. The Authentic Leadership Questionnaire 1.0 rater version with 16 items and a Personal Data Sheet were additional survey instruments used to collect data in this research study. Approximate completion time for the entire questionnaire was 20 minutes.

Validity and Reliability

Validity

Items in the Spiritual Leadership Survey have been pretested and validated in other studies and samples including discussions with practitioners concerning face validity (Malone & Fry, 2003). Development and validation of items measuring effective organizational commitment and productivity were supported by research conducted by Nyhan (2000).

Walumba et al. (2008) developed methods to assess the Authentic Leadership Questionnaire based on the Multifactor Leadership Questionnaire. The researchers examined differences between authentic leadership, ethical leadership, and transformational leadership. Results from the study determined that authentic leadership is a high order construct confirming arguments by Avolio & Gardner (2005) for authentic leadership as a root construct of leadership. These significant discoveries support the ability to discriminate authentic leadership from other forms of leadership including ethical and transformational. In addition, Walumba et al. (2008) reported a positive relationship regarding follower perception of the leaders' authenticity to individual follower job satisfaction and job performance.

Qualitative research conducted by Endrissat, Muller, and Kaudela-Baum, (2007) used narrative interviews to examine the validity of authentic leadership. Results from this study suggest a clear distinction of the construct of authentic leadership from other leadership forms such as ethical and transformational. Therefore, empirical evidence supports authentic leadership as unique among current leadership models.

Reliability

Prior to use in research studies, questionnaires, and surveys should be assessed for reliability and validity using a systematic approach. A thorough review of the literature provides evidence of reliability statistics from published research studies that have used the questionnaire or survey instrument (Polit & Beck, 2004). A reliable measurement procedure produces the same or similar results when the same individuals or groups are measured under the same conditions (Gravetter & Wallnau, 2005).

The Spiritual Leadership Survey contains seven scales that indicate adequate coefficient alpha reliabilities between .83 and .93. Specific coefficient alphas for each scale are included in the study conducted by Fry, Vitucci and Cedillo (2005). At least 1200 employees participating in studies including schools (Malone & Fry, 2003), military units (Fry, Vitucci, & Cedillo, 2005), cities (Fry, Nisieiwcz, Vitucci, & Cedillo, 2007), police (Fry, Nisieiwcz, & Vitucci, 2007), and for-profit organizations (Fry & Slocum, 2008) confirm the reliability and validity of the spiritual leadership model (International Institute for Spiritual Leadership, 2010). However, additional evidence is required to establish validity for each chosen instrument in this research study.

Data Analysis

Basic data analysis involves "reducing accumulated data to a manageable size, developing summaries, looking for patterns, and applying statistical techniques" (Cooper &Schindler, 2008, p. 34). The quantitative method, included use of correlational analysis, that determined if the same or different constructs existed when comparing The Spiritual Leadership Survey and The Authentic Leadership Questionnaire after surveying 83 volunteers at different mega-church organizations in Houston, Texas. According to Creswell (2009), quantitative researchers seek relationships between variables, prediction, and generalization of findings. Therefore, correlational analysis served as the statistical approach that analyzed interrelationships among multiple variables in both leadership surveys. Arrangement of data in the form of correlations, using a correlation matrix, supported a correlational analysis using data reduction statistics that determined the type, direction, and strength of relationships between variables. Simon and Francis (2004) caution researchers by emphasizing that correlation studies do not determine cause and effect. However, in relation to the proposed study, application of correlational analysis as a data reduction method provided the opportunity to detect structure in relationships between variables resulting in classification of those variables. Results of correlational analysis allowed explanation of variables in addition to identification of specific constructs of interest.

Results from statistical testing will either reject or accept the null hypothesis that The Spiritual Leadership Survey was measuring the same constructs as a secular survey in the form of The Authentic Leadership Questionnaire. Still, results may indicate support for the alternate hypothesis suggesting that The Spiritual Leadership Survey measures different constructs than The Authentic Leadership Questionnaire. Both research instruments have evidence of significant reliability and validity that add credibility to this research.

Summary

Chapter 3 provided details of research methodology for conducting this dissertation study. A quantitative approach provided the method to study constructs in The Spiritual Leadership Survey and the Authentic Leadership Questionnaire using volunteers currently providing services in mega-church organizations in Houston, Texas.

This chapter included recommendations and justification for the correlational research design, research question, hypotheses, proposed population, survey instruments, and plans for data collection, analysis and established validity data. Data obtained from this research study may not be generalizable and replicable to diverse organizations in the business community because of the use of a non-probability snowball sampling method with a risk of sampling bias. Selection of volunteers occurred because of no accessibility. Permission to administer surveys to a random sample of full-time employees was denied to the researcher by every non-denominational mega-church located in Houston, Texas. The following chapters will present a detailed analysis of research results, interpretation, and recommendations.

CHAPTER 4

Results

The purpose of the research study was to determine if the same or different constructs existed by comparing The Spiritual Leadership Survey and The Authentic Leadership Questionnaire. The research procedure was quantitative with a correlational design. The quantitative method offered an opportunity for explanation of any possible associations among constructs. The correlational design provided statistical procedures to measure the degree of association (or relationship) between two or more variables using correlational analysis (Creswell, 2005). Participants were volunteers, age 18 and older, in mega-church organizations located in the city of Houston, Texas. Participants completed The Spiritual Leadership Survey and The Authentic Leadership Questionnaire that provided responses concerning knowledge, observations, and experience with leaders and leadership influences in mega-church organizations. The quantitative method was most appropriate for this research study to explain any possible association among constructs part of The Spiritual Leadership Survey and Authentic Leadership Questionnaire. The correlational design was the optimum choice for this specific research since "correlational designs are procedures in quantitative research in which investigators measure the degree of association between variables" (Creswell, 2005, p. 18). Responses from The Spiritual Leadership Survey (Survey A) and the Authentic Leadership Questionnaire (Survey B) were organized in a format to calculate several bivariate Pearson Product-Moment Correlation Coefficients (r) simultaneously using the SPSS statistical program. Significant correlations were displayed as a correlation matrix. The strength and direction of each correlation occurred after examination of significant correlations ($p < .05$). Correlational analysis determined if a relationship existed among constructs associated with The Spiritual Leadership Survey (Survey A) and The Authentic Leadership Questionnaire (Survey B). Initial patterns among variables were analyzed in a correlation matrix, (b) variables were reduced from a large number to smaller number of factors, and (c) hypotheses were tested to arrive at conclusions.

Chapter one presented the background of the current leadership crisis in the United States, the specific problem to be studied, purpose of the study, conceptual framework, and the academic and social significance of the research. Chapter two provided a review of the current literature regarding the paradigm shift among leadership models, evolution of leadership, history of spiritual leadership, authentic leadership and description of mega-church organizations.

Chapter two also reviewed controversies in the literature regarding spiritual leadership followed by suggestions of how spiritual leadership is one of the most viable alternatives to address the leadership crisis. Chapter three presented recommendations and justification for the quantitative method, and correlational research design, research questions, hypothesis, proposed population, survey instruments, plans for data collection, analysis and established validity data. Chapter four presents the demographics, data collection, research method, analysis, results, interpretation, and recommendations.

Research Question and Hypotheses

The primary research question and hypotheses were posed to determine if the same or different constructs existed between The Spiritual Leadership Survey and The Authentic Leadership Questionnaire.

R1: Does the Spiritual Leadership Survey measure the same or different constructs than The Authentic Leadership Questionnaire for volunteers in mega-churches located in Houston, Texas?

Hypotheses were developed to measure the strength of association among constructs concerning Spiritual Leadership and Authentic Leadership. From this research question, the null hypothesis states:

Ho: The Spiritual Leadership Survey measures the same constructs as the Authentic Leadership Questionnaire for volunteers in mega-churches located in Houston, Texas.

An alternative hypothesis from the research question states:

H1: The Spiritual Leadership Survey measures different constructs than The Authentic Leadership Questionnaire for volunteers in mega-churches located in Houston, Texas.

Data Collection Procedures

Electronic data collection methods were used for this study as a means to address the research question. Permission from the authors of the Spiritual Leadership Survey and Authentic Leadership Questionnaire were obtained to compile research data for the current study (see Appendix B and D). Each validated survey provided responses used to measure the degree of relationship between constructs associated with spiritual and authentic leadership.

Volunteers at each mega-church organization were sent an electronic version of the cover letter, informed consent, Spiritual Leadership Survey and Authentic Leadership Questionnaire to their personal e-mail address. A random sample of 100 full-time employees could not be obtained because permission to administer surveys was denied to the researcher by every non-denominational mega-church located in the city of Houston, Texas. Demographic data and valid responses from each survey were gathered from a non-probability snowball sample of 100 volunteers at mega-church organizations located in Houston, Texas. The initial response to survey invitations resulted in 30 participants. The sample size increased to 83 but fell short of the 100 anticipated responses from volunteers in the mega-church organizations. A total of 83 responses were obtained or 83%.

Each participant in the survey was assigned a unique code with no other information to identify the individual. After closure of the designated data collection period surveys were organized according to specific codes and saved in a password protected database. The data were analyzed applying score means, medians, percentages, frequencies, and ranges.

Data Demographics

100 volunteers were referred to complete the surveys; however, 17 either did not complete the survey or failed to meet the criteria. The remaining 83 volunteers responded to all questions and completed each survey. Of the 83 participants 21.5% were male and 47.3% were female with the mean age range being, 31 to 40 as seen in Figure 1.

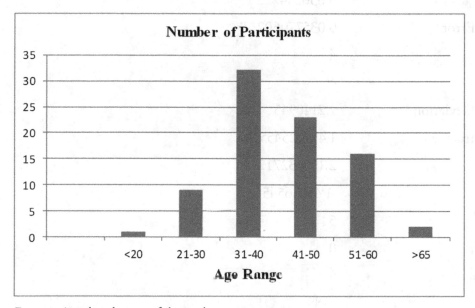

Figure 1. Age distribution of the study participants.

Twenty-seven percent of the participants reported an income of over $50,000 per year. Thirty-four percent of the participants reported college graduate level education. Eighty-three percent of the participants reported volunteer status in their mega-church organizations.

The data analysis will only describe if a correlation or relationship exists among variables in The Spiritual Leadership Survey and Authentic Leadership Questionnaire. No manipulation occurred by the researcher regarding an independent or dependent variable. The terms independent and dependent variable will not be used in the description of a correlational study that only examines the possibility of a relationship among variables. The results describing only the most distinct patterns will be included in the data analysis section. Statistically significant relationships do not imply cause and effect but merely an association among variables. Results do not indicate that Spiritual Leadership constructs causes changes at individual or organizational levels.

Data Analysis

Statistics including the mean, standard deviation, variance, range, frequency and level of significance are summarized in Table 1 for The Spiritual Leadership Survey (Survey A) and Authentic Leadership Questionnaire (Survey B).

Table 1

Survey A and Survey B Summary Statistics

Mean	3.636284722
Standard Error	0.035770602
Median	4
Mode	4
Standard Deviation	1.2140945
Sample Variance	1.474025455
Kurtosis	2.199632712
Skewness	-1.45036545
Range	5
Minimum	0
Maximum	5
Sum	4189
Count	1152
Confidence Level (95.0%)	0.070182893

Responses from The Spiritual Leadership Survey (Survey A) and the Authentic Leadership Questionnaire (Survey B) were organized in a format to calculate several bivariate Pearson Product-Moment Correlation Coefficients (r) simultaneously using the SPSS statistical program. Significant correlations were displayed as a correlation matrix. The strength and direction of each correlation occurred after examination of significant correlations ($p < .05$).

Initial results of the correlational analysis, from an SPSS software program, summarized correlation coefficients in a table. The Spiritual Leadership Survey (Survey A) consisted of 18 Likert-scale questions (1=Strongly Disagree 2=Disagree 3=Neither Agree or Disagree 4=Agree 5=Strongly Agree) while the Authentic Leadership Questionnaire (Survey B) consisted of 16 Likert-scale questions (0=Not at all 1=Once in a while 2=Sometimes 3=Fairly Often 4= Frequently if not Always). Numeric responses from each participant were calculated and placed in a 34X34 correlation matrix. A confidence interval of 95% was used to accept or reject the study's hypotheses. To achieve 95% confidence with 83 data points (*n*=83) the Pearson correlation – coefficient r value must be greater than 0.220. Correlation matrix results indicated "this matrix is not positive definite." Tabachnick & Fidell (2007) recommended review of the correlation matrix for correlation coefficients over 0.30. Table 2 indicated multiple correlations that did not exceed 0.30. Pairs of correlations were examined to determine what meaningful information could be obtained to address the strength of association among variables.

Table 2 represents a summary of significant correlations from The Spiritual Leadership Survey (Survey A) and Authentic Leadership Questionnaire (Survey B). Significant correlations were summarized in a reduced format from the larger correlation matrix. Survey A factors were paired to each of the Survey B factors from a total sample of 83 participants.

Table 2

Significant Correlation Summary – $p < .05$, two tails, n=83

	B1	B2	B3	B4	B5	B6	B7	B8	B9
A2 Pearson Correlation Sig (2-tailed) N=83									.231* .036 83
A5 Pearson Correlation Sig (2-tailed) N=83					.246* .025 83		.274* .012 83		
A6 Pearson Correlation Sig (2-tailed) N=83				.263* .016 83					

A7 Pearson Correlation Sig (2-tailed) N=83						.251* .022 83		.269* .014 83
A9 Pearson Correlation Sig (2-tailed)				.230* .037 83	.229* .037 83			
A10 Pearson Correlation Sig (2-tailed) N=83							.278* .011 83	
A13 Pearson Correlation Sig (2-tailed) N=83		.233* .034 83			.259* .018 83	.266* .015 83		.251* .022 83
A14 Pearson Correlation Sig (2-tailed) N=83		.231* .036 83					.246* .025 83	
A15 Pearson Correlation Sig (2-tailed) N=83	.274* .012 83				.242* .028 83	.274* .012 83		

*Correlation is significant at the 0.05 level (2-tailed)

Table 3 includes participant's paired responses for variables in The Spiritual Leadership, Survey A (Vision, Hope/Faith, Altruistic Love, Meaning/Calling, Membership, Inner Life, Organizational Commitment, Productivity, Satisfaction with Life) and variables in The Authentic Leadership Questionnaire including (Transparency, Moral/Ethical, Balanced Processing, Self-Awareness). All correlations for variables associated with The Spiritual Leadership Survey and Authentic Leadership Questionnaire were significant ($p < .05$, $\alpha = .05$). The direction for all correlations was positive, but the strengths of the correlations were weak to very weak for variables associated among spiritual leadership and authentic leadership.

Table 3

Significant Correlations for Spiritual and Authentic Leadership

Variables	r	p< .05 *two tails	n=83
A2 (Vision)			
B9 (Moral/Ethical)	.231	.036*	n=83
A5 (Altruistic Love)			
B5 (Transparency)	.246	.025*	n=83
A5 (Altruistic Love)			
B7 (Moral/Ethical)	.274	.012*	n=83
A6 (Altruistic Love)			
B4 (Transparency)	.263	.016*	n=83
A7 (Meaning/Calling)			
B6 (Moral/Ethical)	.251	.022*	n=83
A7 (Meaning/Calling)			
B9 (Moral/Ethical)	.269	.014*	n=83
A9 (Membership)			
B5 (Transparency)	.230	.037*	n=83
A9 (Membership)			
B6 (Moral/Ethical)	.229	.037*	n=83
A10 (Membership)			
B7 (Moral Ethical)	.278	.011*	n=83
A13 (Organizational Commitment)			
B2 (Transparency)	.233	.034*	n=83
A13 (Organizational Commitment)			
B5 (Transparency)	.259	.018*	n=83
A13 (Organizational Commitment)			
B7 (Moral/Ethical)	.266	.015*	n=83
A13 (Organizational Commitment)			

Dr. Pamela Allen

B9 (Moral/Ethical)	.251	.022*	n=83
A14 (Organizational (Commitment)			
B2 (Transparency)	.231	.036*	n=83
A14 (Organizational (Commitment)			
B8 (Moral/Ethical)	.246	.025*	n=83
A15 (Productivity)			
B1 (Transparency)	.274	.012*	n=83
A15 (Productivity)			
B6 (Moral/Ethical)	.242	.028*	n=83
A15 (Productivity)			
B7 (Moral/Ethical)	.274	.012*	n=83

Findings

Hypothesis

Ho: The Spiritual Leadership Survey measures the same constructs as the Authentic Leadership Questionnaire for volunteers in mega-churches located in Houston, Texas.

H1: The Spiritual Leadership Survey measures different constructs than The Authentic Leadership Questionnaire for volunteers in mega-churches located in Houston, Texas.

The Null hypothesis focused on determining the degree of association among constructs found in The Spiritual Leadership Survey and Authentic Leadership Questionnaire. The initial step in the correlational analysis resulted in development of a correlation matrix for all variables related to both surveys. The most significant correlations were placed in a separate table to determine the strength of association regarding more specific variables. A confidence interval of 95% was used to accept or reject the study's hypothesis. To achieve 95% confidence with 83 data points (n=83) the critical value table for Pearson's Correlation Coefficient indicated the r value must be greater than 0.217 or less than -0.217 (Triola, 2001). The Null hypothesis was rejected because despite significant correlations, $p < .05$, α .05, degrees of association were weak to very weak. The Spiritual Leadership Survey does not measure the same constructs as the Authentic Leadership Questionnaire.

Summary

Two hypotheses were tested to determine whether the Spiritual Leadership Survey measured the same or different constructs than the Authentic Leadership Questionnaire. Survey data were collected from volunteers in mega-church organizations. All possible relationships between the variables were summarized in a correlation matrix containing significant correlations. Correlation matrix results indicated "this matrix is not positive definite." Hypothesis tests found weak to very weak associations among variables in The Spiritual Leadership Survey and Authentic Leadership Questionnaire. The Null hypothesis was rejected regarding The Spiritual Leadership Survey measuring the same constructs as the Authentic Leadership Questionnaire. The Alternate hypothesis is accepted that The Spiritual Leadership Survey measures different constructs than the Authentic Leadership Questionnaire. Chapter 5 includes a discussion regarding meaningful results, possible implications, and recommendations for further consideration.

CHAPTER 5

Conclusions and Recommendations

The current crisis in leadership continues to provide reflections of abandoning ethical business practices, standards of integrity, public accountability, and moral reasoning that influence individuals and groups to rationalize lies and deceit (Fry & Slocum, 2008; Dealy & Thomas, 2006; Walumba et al. 2008). Systematic changes on intrinsic and extrinsic levels suggest a *cultural-spiritual* shift in corporate consciousness (Scharmer, 2009). Limited empirical evidence is available to support this proposition.

The objective of this research was to determine if constructs associated with Spiritual Leadership were the same or significantly different from constructs associated with Authentic Leadership. The study used a quantitative method and correlational analysis to determine the degree of association among Spiritual Leadership and Authentic Leadership. The study's population included volunteers from mega-church organizations located in Houston, Texas. The sampling frame consisted of 83 adult males and females ages 18 and older. The terms independent and dependent variable were not included in the research study. Correlational research does not involve control or systematic variation of variables. Causal language is more common in experimental and quasi-experimental studies. A causal relationship will not be implied or stated because significant relationships were found in this correlational study.

The primary research question guiding this study inquired if the Spiritual Leadership Survey measured the same or different constructs than The Authentic Leadership Questionnaire for volunteers in mega-churches located in Houston, Texas. One null and alternative hypothesis addressed the research objective. The hypothesis sought to determine the degree of association among constructs associated with The Spiritual Leadership Survey and Authentic Leadership Questionnaire. Initial steps from a correlational analysis included statistical methods used to arrive at significant findings.

Three limitations affected this study. First, initial data collection involved use of a non-probability snowball sampling method because requests to administer surveys to the population of full-time employees in the entire population of non-denominational mega- churches located in Houston, Texas were denied to the researcher of this study. Second, the process for selection involved a snowball sampling technique and not random selection. Volunteers from mega-church organizations completed surveys and referred other volunteers willing to participate in the research study. Social desirability is a bias to consider because volunteers in a mega church environment may respond according to what is socially desirable. Third, a larger sample size would have been preferred but only a small sample size below 100 could be obtained at the time of the study due to time constraints. The following section provides conclusions of the study, summary of research findings, literature review, and research methodology. Following the conclusions is a discussion of implications and recommendations.

Conclusions

The study found weak associations among variables in The Spiritual Leadership Survey and Authentic Leadership Questionnaire. Two primary conclusions can be determined from these results. First, The Spiritual Leadership Survey measures different constructs than The Authentic Leadership Survey. Second, The Spiritual Leadership Survey is capable of identifying variables associated with spiritual leaders in mega-church organizations that influence a unique type of commitment among volunteers.

The first conclusion that The Spiritual Leadership Survey measures different constructs than the Authentic Leadership Questionnaire supports prior research that addresses this issue. Empirical evidence included in research conducted by Podsakoff, Mackenzie, Podsakoff & Lee (2003) and Fry (2003) proposed that spiritual leadership theory supports foundational concepts of transformational, charismatic, servant, authentic, and path-goal theories of leadership but spiritual leadership concepts are very distinct. Formation of the spiritual leadership theory included structural equation model techniques, and confirmatory factor modeling with reflective indicators to avoid problems that established transformational or charismatic leadership theories had with theoretical or measurement model misspecifications (Fry, Vitucci & Cedillo, 2005). Structural Equation Modeling that includes confirmatory factor analysis is one of the most rigorous quantitative methodological approaches for testing the validity of factors (Blyne, 2001).

The second conclusion that The Spiritual Leadership Survey is capable of identifying variables associated with spiritual leaders in mega-church organizations that influence a unique type of commitment among volunteers supports reports from other contemporary scholars regarding a significant causal relationship between leadership, spirituality, and organizational commitment (Sanders, Hopkins, & Geroy, 2005). Recommendations in current literature suggest a re-invention of leadership focusing on the well-being of people, psychological well-being, ethical well-being, sense of purpose, meaning, calling, spiritual, moral, authentic, transparent, and socially responsible demonstrations of behavior (Fry & Slocum, 2008; Walumbwa, Avolio, Gardner, Wernsing, & Peterson, 2008; Sendjaya, 2007; Pauchant, 2005). Results of a multi-method study by vanKnippenberg and vanKnippenberg (2005) found enhanced levels of productivity and ratings associated with effective leadership when self-sacrifice, as a construct of spiritual leadership, was applied in lab, scenario, and survey experiments.

Detection of statistical relationships requires that variables change in association or relationship with one another (Triola, 2001). The mean for Survey A was 4.2 with a standard deviation of 0.7 while the mean for Survey B was 3.0 with a standard deviation of 1.2. The mean for Survey A and B was 3.6 with a standard deviation of 1.2 (see Table 1). All correlations for variables associated with The Spiritual Leadership Survey and Authentic Leadership Questionnaire were significant ($p < .05$, $\alpha = .05$). The direction for all correlations was positive, but the strengths of the correlations were weak for variables associated with spiritual leadership and authentic leadership. Discussions of the rationale for these conclusions are included in the hypothesis section.

Hypothesis I

The null and alternative hypotheses focused on determining the degree of association among constructs found in The Spiritual Leadership Survey and Authentic Leadership Questionnaire. Research literature supported additional assessments to establish discriminant validity (Walumbwa, Avolio, Gardner, Wernsing & Peterson, 2008; Markow & Klenke, 2005). Low correlations between The Spiritual Leadership and Authentic Leadership Questionnaire established discriminant validity considering weak associations among multiple scales associated with (altruistic love and membership) in the Spiritual Leadership Survey and (moral/ethical behavior and transparency) associated with the Authentic Leadership Questionnaire. The degree of association among, theoretically related, variables among each survey were considered weak to very weak.

Central to spiritual leadership is the experience of leaders and followers to have a sense of calling, meaningful life, and making a difference (Fry, 2008). Spiritual leadership emphasizes care and concern for self and others that creates a social/organizational culture supporting values of altruistic love, membership, understanding and appreciation (Fry, 2008). Followers need motivation to continue hope toward the future. Spiritual leadership generates faith in the organization's vision that satisfies the essential need that supports continual organizational productivity.

Although leader/follower development is also supported by Authentic Leadership underlying constructs suggest a pattern of leader behavior supported by spiritual leadership theory remains distinct. Authentic leadership constructs promote positive psychological capacity and ethical climate, greater self-awareness, internal moral perspective, balanced information processing, leader transparency in relationship to followers and fostering demonstration of positive self-development (Walumbwa et al. 2008). The distinction between spiritual and authentic leadership behaviors is critical in mega-church corporations consisting of 10 to 20 assistant ministers, 30 to 250 full-time staff, at least 2000 volunteers and a yearly budget of at least two million from the smallest organizations (Thumma & Bird, 2008). Identification of distinct spiritual leaders provides additional opportunities to observe spirit led business, leadership behaviors, decision-making and influence upon followers in one of the most successful organizational environments of the 21st century.

Leadership Implications

Paradigm shifts for twenty-first century leaders include roles as social artists, spiritual visionaries, and cultural innovators (Karakas, 2007). The evolution of business leaders supports personal growth and transformation resulting in making a positive difference, authentic enthusiasm, and acknowledgement of love and concern (Karakas, 2007). Recommendations in current literature suggest a re-invention of leadership focusing on the well-being of people, psychological well-being, ethical well-being, sense of purpose, meaning, calling, spiritual, moral, authentic, transparent, and socially responsible demonstrations of behavior (Fry & Slocum, 2008; Walumbwa, Avolio, Gardner, Wernsing, & Peterson, 2008; Sendjaya, 2007; Pauchant, 2005).

Growing interest in spirituality over the past decade provides an opportunity for organizational scholars to consider incorporating measurements of spirituality in assessment of healthy work environments (King & Crowther, 2004). Fry and Slocum (2008) propose top managers need to maximize the triple bottom line or people, planet, and profit by drawing from sources of workplace spirituality, spiritual leadership and conscious capitalism. Post-modern organizations have an opportunity to explore how mega-church business models demonstrate effective leadership, growth, innovation, and profit despite a downturn in the economy (Thumma & Bird, 2008). Study of the spiritual leadership model supports the identification of spiritual leadership as a factor contributing to the success of multiple disciplines including at least 1200 employees participating in studies including schools (Malone & Fry, 2003), military units (Fry, Vitucci, & Cedillo, 2005), cities (Fry, Nisieiwcz, Vitucci, & Cedillo, 2007), police (Fry, Nisieiwcz, & Vitucci, 2007), and for-profit organizations (Fry & Slocum, 2008). Mega-churches as the fastest growing and sustainable corporations in the United States can be added to the emerging research supporting spiritual leadership.

Recommendations

Spiritual leadership theory incorporates and extends transformational, charismatic, ethics, authentic, and servant-leadership theories yet significant constructs remain distinct (Fry, 2008). Recommendations in current literature suggest a

re-invention of leadership focusing on the well-being of people, psychological well-being, ethical well-being, sense of purpose, meaning, calling, spiritual, moral, authentic, transparent, and socially responsible demonstrations of behavior (Fry & Slocum, 2008; Walumbwa, Avolio, Gardner, Wernsing, & Peterson, 2008; Sendjaya, 2007; Pauchant, 2005). Growing interest in spirituality over the past decade provides an opportunity for organizational scholars to consider incorporating measurements of spirituality in assessment of healthy work environments (King & Crowther, 2004).

The results of this study suggest that the distinct constructs of the Spiritual Leadership Survey are significant factors in identifying spiritual versus authentic leaders. The ability for adaptation to unpredictability and orienting the entire organization around meeting ongoing changes in customer needs and demands defines the mega-business entity (Mintzberg, Lampel, Quinn, & Ghoshal, 2003) that has not included the addition of spiritual leaders. Research results merit further study of spiritual leadership in practice.

Recommendations for future research

1. Replication of this study including employees of mega-churches is recommended. Larger randomized sample sizes would improve the ability to further define observations of Spiritual Leadership in a unique corporate environment. The model of a new spiritual leadership paradigm for mega-church corporations could be developed as a unique organizational form.

2. Spiritual leadership also suggests use of qualitative methodologies to explore spiritual and emotional intelligence as a distinct construct related to spirit-led leaders (Burke, 2006). Zohar and Marshall (2004) support defining great leadership by the reflection of "spiritual capital." They emphasize that spiritually intelligent leadership requires a radical change in prior philosophies and practices of leadership in business. Spiritual leadership includes intelligence of the mind, heart, and spirit. They suggest that future research regarding spiritual leadership include spiritual intelligence as an essential piece. The new millennium will support development of spiritual intelligence that fosters ability to access authentic purpose and self (Scharmer, 2009).

3. Future research regarding psychological capital and spiritual leadership should be explored to determine if a correlation exists with psychological capital. Recent research by Caza, Bagozzi, Woolley, Levy, and Caza (2010) regarding psychological capital and authentic leadership revealed a positive correlation between the two constructs. Future research should include the addition of spiritual leadership.

4. Fry (2005) included employees from multiple disciplines as a part of the research regarding spiritual leadership. However, quantitative and qualitative research involving entrepreneurs would also benefit from exploring perceptions of modeling spiritual leadership and demonstrating spiritual maturity through the business development process.

5. Qualitative research should also explore how spiritual leaders develop and demonstrate transformation at individual and organizational levels over time. How spiritual leadership has been manifested in practice would be a valuable contribution to the diverse community of business, educational, health and science communities. Mega-church corporations would be an optimal choice for further investigation.

6. Research regarding spiritual leadership should extend to more culturally diverse settings. Extensive insights would be obtained by extending beyond the Western perspective to determine cultural influences on spiritual leadership theory, spiritual leadership practice, spiritual intelligence, spirit-led business, spiritual development and transformation.

Summary

This research has practical implications for leaders and organizations interested in confronting the current crisis in leadership regarding leadership ethics (Avolio & Walumbwa, 2006) and leadership accountability (Dealy & Thomas, 2006). Results from this study indicated significant differences among constructs in The Spiritual Leadership Survey versus Authentic Leadership Questionnaire. Benefits of these findings suggest The Spiritual Leadership Survey provides a valid means of identifying spiritual leaders who actually demonstrate how this unique approach contributes to a renewed focus on the well-being of people, psychological well-being, ethical well-being, sense of purpose, meaning, calling, and spiritual, moral, authentic, transparent and socially responsible behaviors. Organizations seeking to provide spiritual leadership development training could incorporate the Spiritual Leadership Survey into the design. But, combining spiritual, authentic, ethical and transformational leadership models into the training would also determine if other leadership styles exist within the organizational framework. Additional value should include study of spiritual leadership in one of the fastest growing and sustainable corporations in the 21st century.

The Hartford Institute for Religion Research, in partnership with Hartford Seminary and Leadership Network, gathered at least a decade of information exploring the mega church phenomenon in 2000, 2005 and 2008 (Hartford Institute for Religion Research, 2008). Examinations of summaries from each extensive survey propose a shift from the shopping mall concept to mega-corporate model with numerous leadership styles. Development of a mega-church corporate model could be constructed as a new organizational form that includes spiritual leadership and other leadership styles.

Repeated observations of spiritual leaders including qualitative and quantitative data collection provides opportunities to describe more practical demonstrations of spiritual leadership and influence on followers' attitudes and behaviors. This research suggests additional development of the spiritual leadership survey structure including a version focusing on the leadership perspective and an alternative version focusing on the follower's perspective as a balance to measuring and identifying key characteristics that influence and transform individuals and the organization.

Spiritual leadership offers the new alternative for doing business in corporate America (Fry & Matherly, 2006). The new millennium supports development of spiritual intelligence that fosters ability to access authentic purpose and self (Scharmer, 2009). The mega-church is the new corporation of the 21st century, challenging leaders to join what Scharmer (2009) describes as a *cultural-spiritual* shift toward the rise of a new consciousness in models of leadership.

References

Aguilera, R. V. (2005). Corporate governance and director accountability: An institutional comparative perspective. *British Journal of Management, 16,* S39-S53. doi:10.1111/j.1467-8551.2005.00446.x

Al Arkoubi, K. (2008). *Spiritual leadership and identity in Moroccan business: An ethnographic study of Ynna Holding* (Doctoral dissertation). Available from Dissertations and Theses database. (UMI No. 3338050)

Ashar, H., & Lane-Maher, M. (2004). Success and spirituality in the new business paradigm. *Journal of Management Inquiry, 13*(3). doi:10.1177/1056492604268218

Ashmos, D. P., & Duchon, D. (2000). Spirituality at work: A conceptualization an measure. *Journal of Management Inquiry, 9*(2), 134-145. doi:10.1177/105649260092008

Avolio, B. J. (2005). *Leadership development in balance: Made/born.* Mahwah, NJ: Lawrence Erlbaum.

Avolio, B. J. (2007). Promoting more integrative strategies for leadership theory-building. *American Psychologist, 62*(1), 25-33. doi: 10.1037/0003-066X.62.1.25

Avolio, B. J., & Gardner, W. L. (2005). Authentic leadership development: Getting to the root of positive forms of leadership. *Leadership Quarterly, 16,* 315-338. doi:10.1016/j.leaqua.2005.03.001

Avolio, B. J., Gardner, W. L., & Walumbwa, F. O. (2007). *Authentic leadership questionnaire.* Retrieved from http://www.mindgarden.com/products/alq.htm

Avolio, B. J., & Luthans, F. (2006a). *High impact leader: Moments matter in authentic leadership development.* New York, NY: McGraw-Hill.

Avolio, B. J., & Luthans, F. (2006b). *The high impact leader: Authentic, resilient leadership that gets results and sustains growth.* New York, NY: McGraw-Hill.

Avolio, B. J., & Walumbwa, F. O. (2006). Authentic leadership: Moving HR leaders to a higher level. In J. J. Martocchio (Ed.). *Research in Personnel and Human Resources Management,* (pp. 273-304). Oxford, England, UK: Elsevier/JAI Press.

Benefiel, M. (2005). The second half of the journey: Spiritual leadership for organizational transformation. *The Leadership Quarterly, 16*(5), 723-747. doi:10.1016/j.leaqua.2005.07.005

Biberman, J., & Whitty, M. (1997). A postmodern spiritual future for work. *Journal of Organizational Change Management, 10*(2), 130-138. doi:10.1108/09534819710160790

Biberman, J., & Whitty, M. (2000). *Work and spirit: A reader of new spiritual paradigms for organizations.* Scranton, PA: University of Scranton Press.

Bolman, L. G., & Deal, T. E. (2001). *Leading with soul: An uncommon journey of the spirit.* San Francisco, CA: Jossey-Bass.

Brandt, E. (1996). Corporate pioneers explore spirituality. *HR Magazine, 41*(4), 82-87. doi:10.1177/1350508409104510

Bryan, J. D. (2009). *Team development social networking and its impact on the encouragement of spiritual leadership* (Doctoral dissertation). Available from Dissertations and Theses database. (UMI No. 3350851)

Burack, E. H. (1999). Spirituality in the workplace. *Journal of Organizational Change Management, 12*(4), 280-291. doi:10.1108/02683940210423060

Burke, R. (2006). Leadership and spirituality. *Emerald Group Publishing Limited, 8*(6), 14-25. doi:10.1108/14636680610712504

Cacioppe, R. (2000a). Creating spirit at work: Re-visioning organization development and leadership–part I. *Leadership and Organization Development Journal, 21*(1-2), 48-54. doi:10.1177/1742715010363210

Cacioppe, R. (2000b). Creating spirit at work: Re-visioning organization development And leadership–part II. *Leadership and Organization Development Journal, 21*(1/2), 48-54. doi:10.1108/01437730010318200

Capps, T. E. (2003). Rebuilding trust in corporate America. *Vital Speeches of the Day, 69*(9), 273. Retrieved from http://www.helleniccomserve.com/ ethicalperformance.html

Cash, K. C., Gray, G. R., & Rood, S. A. (2000, August). A framework for accommodating religion and spirituality in the workplace. *The Academy of Management Executive, 14*(3), 124-134.

Cashman, K. (2008). *Leadership from the inside out* (2nd ed.). San Francisco, CA: Berrett-Koehler.

Cavanaugh, G., Hanson, B., Hanson K., & Hinojoso, J. (2001, March). *Toward a spirituality for the contemporary organization: Implications for work, family and society.* Paper presented at the Institute for Spirituality and Organizational Leadership, Santa Clara University, Santa Clara, CA. Retrieved from http://business.scu.edu/ISOL/contemporary_organization.pdf

Cavanagh, G., Hanson, B., Hanson, K., & Hinojoso, J. (2004). *Toward a spirituality for The contemporary organization.* Oxford, England, UK: Elsevier Ltd.

Caza, A., Bagozzi, R. P., Woolley, L., Levy, L., & Caza, B. B. (2010). Psychological capital and authentic leadership measurement, gender, and cultural extension, *Asia-Pacific Journal of Business Administration*, 2(1), 53-70. doi: 10.1108/17574321011028972

Chakraborty, S. K., & Chakraborty, D. (2004) The transformed leader and spiritual psychology: A few insights, *Journal of Organizational Change Management, 17*(2), 194–210. doi:10.1108/09534810410530610

Cisikszentmihalyi, M. (2003). *Good business: Leadership, flow and the making of meaning.* New York, NY: Viking Press.

Coles, R. (2000). *Lives of moral leadership.* New York, NY: Random House.

Collins, J. C., & Porras, J. I. (2002). *Built to last: Successful habits of visionary companies.* New York, NY: Harper Collins.

Cone, E. (n.d.). *Mega church mega tech.* Retrieved from http://www.cioinsight.com

Cooper, C., & Nelson, D. (Eds.). (2006). *Positive organizational behavior.* Thousand Oaks, CA: Sage.

Cooper, C. D., Scandura, T. A., & Schriesheim, C. A. (2005). Looking forward from our past: Potential challenges to developing authentic leadership theory and authentic leaders. *The Leadership Quarterly, 16*(3), 475-493. doi:10.1016/j.leaqua.2005.03.008

Cooper, D. R., & Schindler, P. S. (2008). *Business research methods* (10th ed.). New York, NY: McGraw-Hill.

Covey, S. R. (2004). *The 7 habits of highly effective people* (Rev. Ed.). New York, NY: Free Press.

Creswell, J. W. (2003). *Research design: Qualitative, quantitative, and mixed methods approaches* (3rd ed.). Thousand Oaks, CA: Sage.

Creswell, J. W. (2005). *Educational research: Planning, conducting, and evaluating quantitative and qualitative research* (2nd ed.). Upper Saddle River, NJ: Prentice Hall.

Creswell, J. W. (2009). *Research design: Qualitative, quantitative, and mixed methods approaches* (3rd ed.). Thousand Oaks, CA: Sage.

Creswell, J. W., & Plano-Clark, V. L. (2007). *Designing and conducting mixed methods research.* Thousand Oaks, CA: Sage Publications.

Cummings, G. G., Hayduk, I., & Estabrooks, C. (2005). Mitigating the impact of hospital restructuring on nurses: The responsibility of emotionally intelligent leadership. *Nursing Research, 54*(1), 2-12. doi:10.1234/12345678

Dealy, M. D., & Thomas, A. B. (2006). *Managing by accountability: What every leader needs to know about responsibility, integrity, and results.* Westport, CT: Praeger.

Dean, K. L., Fornaciari, C. J., & Mcgee, J. J. (2002). Research in spirituality, religion, and work: Walking the line between relevance and legitimacy. *Academy of Management Proceedings.* doi:10.1108/01437730911003911

Dehler, G. E., & Welsh, M. A. (1994). Organizational transformation: Implications for the new management paradigm. *Journal of Managerial Psychology, 9*(6), 17-26. doi:10.1108/02683949410070179

Delbecq, A. E. (1999). Christian spirituality and contemporary business leadership. *Journal of Organizational Change Management, 12*(4), 345-354. doi:10.1108/09534810810847039

Dent, E. B., Higgins, E., & Wharff, D. M. (2005). Spirituality and leadership: An empirical review of definitions, distinctions and embedded assumptions. *The Leadership Quarterly, 16*(5), 625-653. doi:10.1016/j.leaqua.2005.07.002

Drucker, P. F. (1999). *Management challenges for the 21st century.* New York, NY: Harper Collins.

Duchon, D., & Plowman, D. A. (2005). Nurturing the spirit at work: Impact on work unit performance. *The Leadership Quarterly, 16,* 807-833 doi:10.016/j.leaqua.2005.07.008

Elmes, M., & Smith, C. (2001). Moved by the spirit contextualizing workplace empowerment in American spiritual ideals. *Journal of Applied Behavioral Science, 37*(1), 33-50. doi:10.1177/0021886301371003

Endrissat, N., Muller, W. R., & Kaudela-Baum, S. (2007). En route to an empirically-based understanding of authentic leadership. *European Management Journal, 25*(3). doi:10.1016/j.emj.2007.04.004

Fairholm, G. W. (1996). Spiritual leadership: Fulfilling whole-self needs at work. *Leadership and Organization Development Journal, 17*(5), 11-17. doi:10.110801437739610127469

Fairholm, G. W. (1997). *Capturing the heart of leadership: Spirituality and community in the new American workplace.* Westport, CT: Praeger.

Fairholm, G. W. (1998). *Perspectives on leadership: From the science of management to its spiritual heart.* Westport, CT: Quorum Books.

Fairholm, G. W. (2001). *Mastering inner leadership.* Westport, CT: Quorum Books.

Fowler, F. J. (2009). *Survey research methods* (4th ed.). Thousand Oaks, CA: Sage.

Fry, L. W. (2003). Toward a theory of spiritual leadership. *The Leadership Quarterly, 14*(6), 693-727. doi:10.106/j.leaqua.2003.09.001

Fry, L. W. (2005). Introduction to *The Leadership Quarterly* special issue: Toward a paradigm of spiritual leadership. *The Leadership Quarterly, 16*(5), 619-622. doi:10.1016/j.leaqua.2005.07.001

Fry, L. W., Matherly, L., & Vitucci, S. (2005). *In search of authenticity: Spiritual leadership theory as a source for future theory, research and recovery for workaholism.* In B. Avolio, W. Gardner, & F. Walumbwa (Eds.), Authentic leadership theory and practice: Origins, effects, and development. *Monographs in Leadership and Management, Vol. 3* (pp. 183-200). Retrieved from http://www.iispiritualleadership.com/resources/publications.php

Fry, L. W., & Matherly, L. L. (2006, June). *Spiritual leadership as an integrating paradigm for positive leadership development.* Paper presented at the Gallup International Leadership Summit, Washington DC. Retrieved from http://www.iispiritualleadership.com/resources/papers.php

Fry, L. W., Nisieiwcz, M., & Vitucci, S. (2007, August). *Transforming police organizations through spiritual leadership.* Paper presented at the 2007 Academy of Management, Philadelphia, PA. Retrieved from http://www.iispiritualleadership.com/resources/papers.php

Fry, L. W., Nisieiwcz, M., Vitucci, S., & Cedillo, M. (2007, August). *Transforming city government through spiritual leadership.* Paper presented at the 2007 Academy of Management, Philadelphia, PA. Retrieved from http://www.iispiritualleadership.com/resources/papers.php

Fry, L. W., & Slocum, J. W., Jr. (2008). Maximizing the triple bottom line through spiritual leadership. *Organizational Dynamics, 37*(1), 86-96. doi:10.1016/j.orgdyn.2007.11.004

Fry, L. W., Vitucci, S., & Cedillo, M. (2005). Spiritual leadership and army transformation: Theory, measurement, and establishing a baseline. *The Leadership Quarterly, 16*(5), 835-862. doi:10.1016/j.leaqua.2005.07.012

Fry, L. W., & Whittington, J. L. (2005, August). *Spiritual leadership theory as a paradigm for organizational development and transformation.* Presented at the 2005 National Academy of Management, Honolulu, HI. Retrieved from http://www.iispiritualleadership.com/resources/papers.php

Garger, J. (2008). Developing authentic leadership in organizations: Some insights and observations. *Development and Learning In Organizations, 22*(1), 14-18. doi:10.1108/14777280810840058

Geaney, M. M. (2004). *Spirituality and business transformation: Exploring spirituality with executive leaders* (Doctoral dissertation). Available from ProQuest Dissertations and Theses database. (UMI No. 3133574)

George, B. (2003). *Authentic leadership: Rediscovering the secrets to creating lasting value*. San Francisco, CA: Jossey-Bass.

George, B., & Sims, P. (2007). *True north: Discover your authentic leadership*. San Francisco, CA: Jossey-Bass.

George, B., Sims, P., McLean, A. N., & Mayer, D. (2007). Discovering your authentic leadership. *Harvard Business Review, 85*(2), 129-138. doi:10.1177/0149206307308913

Grant, D., O'Neil, K., & Stephens, L. (2004). Spirituality in the workplace: New empirical directions in the study of the sacred. *Sociology of Religion, 65*(3), 265-283. doi:10.2307/3712252

Gravetter, F. J., & Wallnau, L. B. (2005). *Essentials of statistics for the behavioral sciences* (5th ed.). Belmont, CA: Wadsworth/Thomson Learning.

Hartford Institute for Religion Research. (n.d.). *Mega churches today*. Retrieved from http://hirr. hartsem.edu

Heaton, D. P., Schmidt-Wilk, J., & Travis, F. (2004). Constructs, methods, and measures for researching spirituality in organizations. *Journal of Organizational Change Management, 17*(1), 62-82. doi:10.1108/09534810410511305

Herber, J., Singh, J., & & Useem, M. (2000). The design of new organizational forms. In H. Mintzberg, J. Lampel, J. B. Quinn, & S. Ghoshal. (Eds.). (2003). *The strategy process: Concepts, contexts, cases* (4th ed., pp 234-238). Upper Saddle River, NJ: Prentice Hall.

Hesselbein, F., Goldsmith, M., & Beckhard, R. (2000). *The leader of the future: New visions, strategies and practices for the next era*. San Francisco, CA: Jossey-Bass.

Hicks, D. A. (2002). Spiritual and religious diversity in the workplace: Implications for leadership. *The Leadership Quarterly, 13*(4), 379-396. doi:10.1016/S1048-9843(02)00124-8

Hinton, M. D. (2007). *The visible institution: Theology and religious education in two black mega-church ministries* (Doctoral dissertation). Available from ProQuest Dissertations and Theses database. (UMI No. 3271021)

Holloway, M., & Moss, B. (2010). *Spirituality and social work*. Philadelphia, PA: Jessica Kingsley.

Hoppe, S. L. (2005). Spirituality and leadership: New directions for teaching and Learning. *Wiley Periodicals* (104), 83–92. doi:10.1002/tl.217

Howard, S. (2002). A spiritual perspective on learning in the workplace. *Journal of Managerial Psychology, 17*(3),230-242. doi:10.1108026839402104231132

International Institute for Spiritual Leadership. (2010). *Spiritual leadership*. Retrieved from http://www.iispiritualleadership.com

Irwin, C. E., & Roller, R. H. (2000, September). Pastoral preparation for church management. *Journal of Ministry Marketing & Management, 6*(1), 53-67. doi:10.1300/J093v06n01_05

Jensen, S. M., & Luthans, F. (2006). Entrepreneurs as authentic leaders: Impact on employees' attitudes. *Leadership and Organization Development Journal, 27*(8), 646-666. doi: 10.110801437730610709273

Jimenez, J. M. (2010). *Residential schools effects: How are these affecting current elders' spiritual leadership* (Doctoral dissertation). Available from pro Quest Dissertations and Theses database. (ATT No. MR58700)

Jones, G. R. (2004). *Organizational theory, design, and change.* Upper Saddle River, NJ: Pearson Education.

Karakas, F. (2007). The twenty-first century leader: Social artist, spiritual visionary, and cultural innovator. *Global Business and Organizational Excellence, 26*(3), 44-50. doi:10.1002/joe.20143

King, J. E. & Crowther, M. R. (2004). The measurement of religiosity and spirituality: Examples and issues from psychology. *Journal of Organizational Behavior, 17*(1), 83-101. doi: 10.110809634810410511314

Kinjerski, V., & Skrypnek, B. J. (2004). Defining spirit at work: Finding common ground. *Journal of Organizational Change Management, 17*(1), 26-42. doi: 10.1108/09534810410511288

Kinjerski, V., & Skrypnek, B. J. (2008). Four paths to spirit at work: Journeys of personal meaning, fulfillment, well-being, and transcendence through work. *The Career Development Quarterly, 56*(4), 319-329. Retrieved from http://www.kaizensolutions.org/publications.htm

Klenke, K. (2005). Corporate values as multi-level, multi-domain antecedents of leader behaviors. *International Journal of Manpower, 26*(1), 50-66. doi:10.1108/01437720510587271

Korac-Kakabadse, N., Kouzmin, A., & Kakabadse, A. (2002). Spirituality and leadership praxis. *Journal of Managerial Psychology, 17*(3), 165-182. doi:10.1108/02683940210423079

Kouzes, J. M., & Posner, B. Z. (2007). *The leadership challenge* (4th ed.). San Francisco, CA: Jossey-Bass.

Kuhn, T. S. (1996). *The structure of scientific revolutions* (3rd ed.). Chicago, IL: The University of Chicago Press.

Laing, C. J. (2005). *Spirituality in leadership: A core element in fulfilling mission discovered through appreciative inquiry at St. Paul's Hospital, Royal Roads University, Canada* (Doctoral dissertation). Available from ProQuest Dissertation and Theses database. (AAT No. MR04087)

Levy, R. B. (2000). My experience as participant in the course on spirituality for executive leadership. *Journal of Management Inquiry, 9*(2), 129-131. doi:10.1177/0022167805283776

Lunenburg, F. C. & Irby, B. J. (2008). *Writing a successful thesis or dissertation: Tips and strategies for students in the social and behavioral sciences.* Thousand Oaks, CA: Corwin Press.

Luthans, F., & Avolio, B. J. (2003). Authentic leadership a positive development approach. In K. S. Cameron, J. E. Dutton, & R. E. Quinn (Eds.). *Positive organizational scholarship: Foundations for a new schoalrship,* (pp. 241-258). San Francisco, CA: Berrett-Koehler.

Magnusen, C. L. (2002). Spirituality and leadership effectiveness: Historical and philosophical trends. *Catholic Education: A Journal of Inquiry and Practice, 6*(2), 251-258. Retrieved from http://ejournals.bc.edu/ojs/index.php/catholic/article/ view/979

Malone, P., & Fry, L. W. (2003, August). *Transforming schools through spiritual leadership: A field experiment.* Paper presented at the 2003 National Academy of Management, Seattle, WA. Retrieved from http://www.iispiritualleadership.com/resources/ papers.php

Markow, F., & Klenke, K. (2005). An empirical investigation of spiritual leadership. *International Journal of Organizational Analysis, 13*(1), 8-27. doi:10.1108/eb028995

Marques, J. F. (2008). Spiritual performance from an organizational perspective: The Starbucks way. *Corporate Governance, 8*(3), 248 – 257. doi:10.1108/14720700810879141

Milliman, J. (2008). In search of spiritual leadership: A case study of entrepreneur Steve Bigari. *Business Renaissance Quarterly, 3*(1), 19-41. Retrieved from http://vlex.com/vid/spiritual-entrepreneur-bigari-65007483

Milliman, J., Ferguson, J., Trickett, D., & Condemi, B. (1999). Spirit and community at Southwest Airlines: An investigation of a spiritual values-based model. *Journal of Organizational Change Management, 12*(3), 221-233. doi:10.1108/09534819910273928

Mintzberg, H., Lampel, J., Quinn, J. B., & Ghoshal, S. (Eds.). (2003). *The strategy process: Concepts, contexts, cases* (4th ed.). Upper Saddle River, NJ: Prentice Hall.

Mitroff, I. I., & Denton, E. A. (1999). *A spiritual audit of corporate America: A hard look at spirituality, religion, and values in the workplace.* San Francisco, CA: Jossey-Bass.

Mohamed, A. A., Wisnieski, J., Askar, M., & Syed, I. (1993). Towards a theory of spirituality in the workplace. *Competitiveness Review: An International Business Journal Incorporating Journal of Global Competitiveness, 14*(1/2), 102-107. doi:10.1108/eb046473

Novicevic, M. M., Davis, W., Dorn, F., Buckley, M. R., Brown, J. A. (2005). Barnard on conflicts of responsibility. Implications for today's perspectives on transformational and authentic leadership. *Management Decision, 43*(10), 1396-1409. doi: 10.1108002517405106349 30

Nyhan, R. C. (2000). Changing the paradigm: Trust and its role in public sector organizations. *American Review of Public Administration, 30*(1), 87-109. doi:10.1177/02750740022064560

Onwuegbuzie, A. J., & Leech, N. L. (2005). On becoming a pragmatic researcher: The importance of combining quantitative and qualitative research methodologies. *International Journal of Social Research Methodology, 8*(5), 375-387. doi:10.1080/1364557050042447

Pandey, A., & Gupta, R. (2008). Spirituality in management: A review of contemporary and traditional thoughts and agenda for research. *Global Business Review, 9*(1), 65-83. doi:10.1177/097215090700900105

Pauchant, T.C. (2005). Integral leadership: A research proposal. *Journal of Organizational Change Management, 18*(3), 211-229. doi: 10.110809634810610699380

Pawar, B. S. (2008). Two approaches to workplace spirituality facilitation: A comparison and implications, *Leadership & Organization Development Journal, 29*(6), 544-567. doi:10.1108/01437730810894195

Peters, T., & Waterman, R. (1982). *In search of excellence: Lessons from America's best-run companies.* New York, NY: Harper and Row.

Pfeffer, J. (2003). Business and the spirit: Management practices that sustain values. In R. A. Giacalone & Jurkiewics (Eds.). *The handbook of workplace spirituality and organizational performance* (pp. 29-45). New York, NY: M. E. Sharpe.

Polit, D. F., & Beck, C. T. (2004). *Nursing research: Principles and methods* (7th ed.). Philadelphia, PA: Lippincott, Williams & Wilkins.

Quinnine, T. E. (2007). *Spiritual leadership within the service industry: A phenomenological study interpreting the spiritual leadership experiences of eight business executives* (Doctoral dissertation). Available from ProQuest Dissertations and Theses database. (UMI No. 3264282)

Rojas, R. R. (2002). *Management theory and spirituality: A framework and validation of the independent spirituality assessment scale* (Doctoral dissertation). Available from Dissertation Information Service. (UMI No. 3043030)

Ruschman, N. L. (2002). Servant-leadership and the best companies to work for in America. In L. C. Spears & M. Lawrence (Eds.). *Focus on leadership: Servant leadership for the twenty-first century* (pp. 123-139). New York, NY: John Wiley & Sons.

Sanders, J. E., Hopkins, W. E., & Geroy, G. D. (2003). From transactional to transcendental: Toward an integrated theory of leadership. *Journal of Leadership and Organizational Studies, 9*(4), 21-31. doi:10.1177/107179190300900402

Sanders, J. E., Hopkins, W. E., & Geroy, G. D. (2005). A causal assessment of the spirituality-leadership-commitment relationship. *Journal of Management, Spirituality & Religion, 2*(1), 39-66. doi:

Sarros, J. C., & Cooper, B. K. (2006). Building character: A leadership essential. *Journal of Business and Psychology, 21*(1), 1-22. doi:10.1108/14777260910984014

Scharmer, C. O. (2009). *Theory U: Leading from the future as it emerges.* San Francisco, CA: Berrett-Koehler.

Scott, W. R., & Davis, G. F. (2007). *Organizations and organizing: Rational, natural and open systems perspectives* (4th ed.). Old Tappan, NJ: Pearson.

Sendjaya, S. (2007). *Conceptualizing and Measuring Spiritual Leadership in Organizations, 2*(1), 104-126. doi:

Shirey, M. R. (2006). Authentic leaders creating healthy work environments for nursing practice. *American Journal of Critical Care, 15*(3), 256-287. Retrieved from http://ajcc.aacnjournals.org

Simon, M. K., & Francis, B. J. (2004). *The dissertation cookbook. From soup to nuts: A practical guide to start and complete your dissertation* (3rd ed.). Dubuque, IA: Kendall/Hunt.

Simons, T. (2002). Behavioral integrity: The perceived alignment between manager's words and deeds as a research focus. *Organization Science, 13,* 18-35. doi:10.1287/orsc.13.1.18.543

Smith, S. L. (2007). *Spiritual leadership as an effective leadership style for the public school superintendent* (Doctoral dissertation). Available from ProQuest Dissertations and Theses database. (UMI No. 3292248)

Sproull, N. L. (2002*). Handbook of research methods: A guide for practitioners and students in the social sciences* (2nd ed.). Lanham, MD: Scarecrow Press.

Storr, L. (2004). Leading with integrity: A qualitative research study. *Journal of Health Organization and Management, 18*(6), 415-434. doi:10.1108/14777260410569984

Thomas, T., Schermerhorn, J. R., & Dienhart, J. W. (2004). Strategic leadership of ethical behavior in business. *The Academy of Management Executive, 18*(2), 56-65. Retrieved from http://home.sandiego.edu/povett/docs/msgl_503/ leader_ethic_behave.pdf

Thumma, S. (2001). *Mega churches today.* Retrieved from http://hirr.hartsem.edu/org/faith_megachurches_FACTsummary.html#finances

Thumma, S., & Bird, W. (2008). *Changes in American mega churches: Tracing eight years of growth and innovation in the nation's largest-attendance congregations.* Retrieved from http://hirr.hartsem.edu/megachurch/megastoday2008_ summaryreport.html

Vaill, P. (2000). Introduction to spirituality for business leadership. *Journal of Management Inquiry, 9*(2), 115-116. doi:10.1177/105649260092004

van Knippenberg, B., van Knippenberg, D., De Cremer, D., & Hogg, M. (2004). Research in leadership, self, and identity: A sample of the present and a glimpse of the future. *Leadership Quarterly, 16*(4), 495-499. doi:10.1016/j.leaqua.2005.06.006

Wagner-Marsh, F., & Conley, J. (1999). The fourth wave: The spiritually-based firm. *Journal of Organizational Change Management, 12*(4), 292-301. doi:10.1177/135050840293014

Walumbwa, F. O., Avolio, B. J., Gardner, W. L., Wernsing, T. S., & Peterson, S. J. (2008). Authentic leadership: Development and validation of a theory-based measure. *Journal of Management, 34*(1). doi:10.1177/0149206307308913

Wharff, D. M. (2004). *Expressions of spiritually inspired leadership in the public sector: Calling for a new paradigm in developing leaders* (Unpublished doctoral dissertation). University of Maryland, College Park, MD. Retrieved from http://www.spirit at work.org/library/wharf.pdf

Whittington, J. L. (2004). Corporate executives as beleaguered rulers: The leader's motive matters. *Problems and Perspectives in Management, 3,* 163-169. Retrieved from www.businessperspectives.org/.../2004/ PPM_EN_2004_03_Whittington.pdf

Wong, C., & Cummings, G. (2009). Authentic leadership: A new theory for nursing or back to basics. *Journal of Health Organization and Management, 23*(5), 1477-7266. doi:10.1108/14777260910984014

Young, R. (2006). *The rise of Lakewood Church and Joel Osteen.* New Kensington, PA: Anchor Distributors.

Yukl, G. A. (2009). *Leadership in organizations* (7th ed.). Upper Saddle River, NJ: Prentice Hall.

Zohar, D., & Marshall, I. (2004). *Spiritual capital wealth we can live by.* San Francisco, CA: Berrett-Koehler.